Sacred HARMONY

THE DIVINE DANCE OF LOVE AND RESPECT IN MARRIAGE

Sacred HARMONY

THE DIVINE DANCE OF LOVE AND RESPECT IN MARRIAGE

Where Love Learns to Listen and Respect
Learns to Embrace

John K. Amoah

Dedication

To my wife, Chrystine Bernard-Amoah, thank you for your love, your strength, and your constant encouragement. Our marriage has been my first classroom and my greatest gift. You bring out the best in me and inspire me to grow. This book is because of us.

Table of Contents

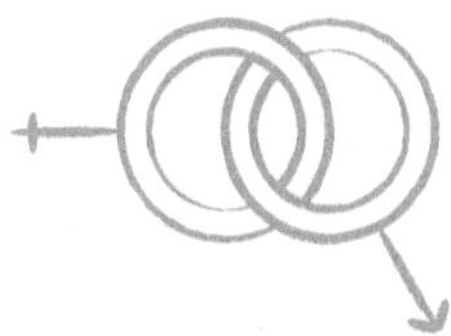

In an era when the meaning of marriage is being redefined, *Sacred Harmony* examines the biblical design of marriage through the key virtues of love and respect. Drawing on Ephesians 5:33, it presents a redemptive picture of marriage as a divine design—one that reflects God's essence through the interplay of love and respect between husband and wife. This book, which draws on Scripture, Ellen G. White's writings, contemporary psychological research, and real-life situations, leads couples through common relational challenges while providing practical strategies for spiritual and emotional closeness. Each chapter combines biblical theology with cutting-edge social science to provide insights into communication, conflict resolution, gender dynamics, sexuality, forgiveness, and legacy building. It teaches couples how to thoroughly understand each other, break destructive cycles, and cultivate a relationship based on mutual honor. The book, written with clarity and affection, addresses couples, pastors, counselors, and educators who want to see Christ-centered relationships thrive across cultures and generations.

Unique Features:

- Scripture-based insights and exegesis
- Reflective worksheets and assessments
- Quotes by Ellen G. White and Christian counselors
- Couple conversation starters
- Prayer prompts
- Discussion prompts

Intended Audience:

The book is intended for Christian couples (particularly young and newly married couples), pastors, family life educators, premarital and marital counselors, and ministry leaders in the Seventh-day Adventist Church and the larger Christian community. It's ideal for group study and marriage getaways.

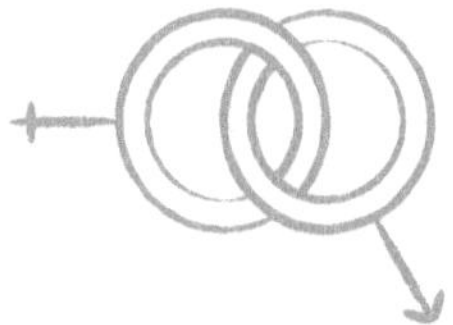

PREFACE

This book was born out of countless conversations. Some emerged in counseling sessions; others poured out in prayer circles, late-night talks between friends, and quiet tears shared in church pews. At the heart of all these stories was one unrelenting cry: "We love each other, but we don't understand each other."

As a minister, family life coach, and student of both Scripture and human behavior, I've witnessed the beauty and the brokenness of marriage. I've seen strong couples crumble under silent resentment and fragile ones rise in faith and flourish. Over and over again, I've seen that when couples begin to understand and meet each other's core emotional needs—a man's need for respect and a woman's need for love—transformation happens.

This truth is not new. It is deeply biblical. It is powerfully human. And it is supported by the best of psychological and sociological research. In Ephesians 5:33, Paul wrote, "Let each one of you in particular so love his own wife as himself, and let the wife see that she respects her husband." This is not a prescription for patriarchy or passivity; it is divine wisdom for harmony.

The idea for this book crystallized during the COVID-19 pandemic when many couples were suddenly confined to the same space for extended periods of time. You would think such proximity would foster greater intimacy, but early research in family life indicates otherwise. Couples began to experience heightened conflict as they spent most of their time at home together. Previously, the busyness of work and daily routines acted as a buffer. But in the stillness of lockdown, the unresolved issues and unmet emotional needs came to the surface. Tension increased. Distance grew. And the question that gnawed on my mind was, "What can I give back to help couples?"

This question led me to launch a virtual family life presentation series every Thursday. Week after week, I listened to participants from various backgrounds share their struggles, questions, and breakthroughs. Their stories, honesty, and hunger for change fueled my burden to write this book—to help the untold thousands of couples silently wrestling with relationship challenges.

In these pages, I have drawn from biblical exposition, the inspired writings of Ellen G. White, the insights of relationship experts like Dr. John Gottman and Dr. Emerson Eggerichs, and the latest research in marriage psychology. But most of all, I have drawn from real people—couples learning to navigate life together in grace and truth.

This book is not meant to be read in haste. It is designed for prayerful reflection, open conversation, and practical application. Whether you read it alone or as a couple, I invite you to listen deeply—to the Spirit of God, to your own heart, and to the heart of your spouse.

If you're tired of misunderstanding…If you long to re-connect…If you want to build a love that lasts…then may this book be a companion on your journey. May it help you hear each other again. See each other again. Cherish each other again.

To every couple who dares to dance in sacred harmony—this is for you.

With gratitude and hope,

John K. Amoah, PhD, DMin, CFLE

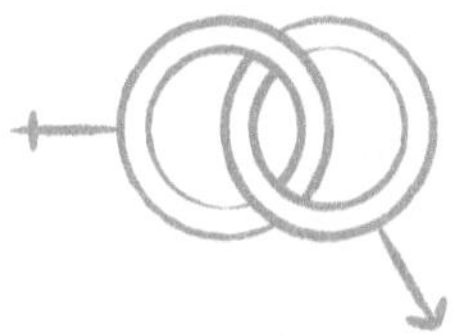

INTRODUCTION:
THE SACRED DANCE BEGINS

Most of us don't fall in love thinking about paperwork or tax brackets. We say yes because something holy stirs in us—the sense that God is inviting two people to build one life. Marriage isn't just a tradition or a promise signed in ink. It's a covenant before God, a calling to reflect His heart together.

Picture a simple scene: keys on the counter, two cups with rings on the table, a half-finished conversation waiting in the air. Real marriage lives there, between errands and bills and little kindnesses. And even in that ordinary space, God designed something extraordinary: a relationship where love and respect move together like melody and harmony. When one rises, the other deepens. When both are present, music fills the room.

But that music can be hard to hear in our world. Roles shift. Social voices grow louder than Scripture. Old hurts follow us into new seasons. Expectations feel unclear. Before long, couples who care deeply about each other can feel miles apart—talking past one another, shutting down, or trying to meet needs they don't fully understand.

Underneath many of those tensions sits a truth that Scripture (Ephesians 5:33) has voiced for centuries and that research echoes today: most men feel strongest and most secure when they are respected; most women feel safest and most open when they are loved well. These aren't shallow preferences. They're woven into how we're made—psychologically, emotionally, and spiritually. When respect dries up, many men lose their confidence and pull back. When love grows thin, many women feel unprotected and close their hearts. But when love and respect show up together, couples don't just cope—they grow.

Sacred Harmony: The Divine Dance of Love and Respect in Marriage is an invitation to hear that music again. Drawing from Scripture, Adventist teaching, relationship science, and honest, real-life stories, we'll explore what husbands and wives most deeply need—and how to give those gifts in ways that honor God and strengthen intimacy.

Along the way you'll see how:

- Respect steadies a man, clarifying his vision, building his courage, and nurturing spiritual leadership.
- Love shelters a woman, creating emotional safety, joy, and trust so she can flourish.
- Conflict, handled with humility, can become a doorway to deeper connection instead of a dead end.
- Prayer, empathy, and quiet acts of service shape the kind of intimacy that lasts.

This isn't theory alone. Each chapter offers reflection prompts and practical assessments you can recognize—moments of misunderstanding, small course corrections, hard-won break-throughs. Whether you're preparing for marriage, a few years in, or decades into a covenant you cherish, you'll find tools you can use right away.

Ellen White reminds us,

"Marriage is something that will influence and affect your life both in this world and in the world to come" (*The Adventist Home*, 43).

That's why this union deserves more than survival mode. It deserves intention, patience, and grace. Our prayer is that as you read, you'll begin to hear God's melody again—the one He composed for your home. May you find your step with each other: love that nourishes, respect that lifts, grace that keeps time, and Christ at the center of it all.

Let the sacred harmony begin.

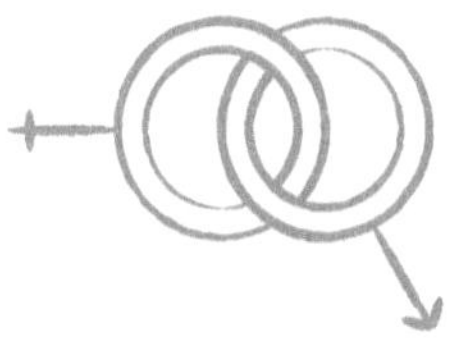

Chapter 1:

SACRED DESIGN—THE DIVINE BLUEPRINT FOR MARRIAGE

"And the LORD God said, 'It is not good that man should be alone; I will make him a helper comparable to him.'"
Genesis 2:18

Marriage didn't begin with a priest at an altar or a government stamp of approval. It wasn't born from tradition or culture. Long before cour-trooms or churches ever existed, marriage was God's idea—conceived in His heart and crafted by His hands.

It's easy to forget that. In today's world, marriage sometimes feels like a contract we negotiate, something practical to manage finances or raise children.

But that's not how it began. Before there was sin, shame, or sorrow, there was union. Two people. One garden. One calling. God created a man and a woman in His image, not to compete, but to complete each other. They weren't thrown together by chance. They were joined in love and purpose.

Marriage is more than romance. It's sacred architecture—heaven's blueprint for companionship, mission, and intimacy.

When God Builds a Relationship

Genesis 2 gives us a picture that's far more intentional than many people realize. Adam wasn't handed a helper like an assistant. He was given someone who reflected his own worth and shared his divine calling.

The Hebrew term *ezer kenegdo*—used to describe Eve—has often been softened in translation. "Helper" sounds small, like someone assisting from the sidelines. But that's not the meaning at all. In the Old Testament, *ezer* is often used to describe God Himself coming to Israel's aid (see Psalm 33:20). It's a word that implies strength, protection, and support. It means *someone who comes alongside with power*.

That means Eve wasn't created to follow Adam from behind, nor to lead him from ahead. She was formed from his side, to walk with him. As Ellen White put it:

> "Eve was created from a rib taken from the side of Adam, signifying that she was not to control him as the head, nor to be trampled under his feet as an inferior, but to stand by his side as an equal" (*Patriarchs and Prophets*, 46).

That one sentence contains more truth than many relationship books. God never designed marriage as a power struggle. He designed it as a **partnership**, rooted in equality, shaped by love, and sustained by grace. Unity without losing individuality. Distinction without division.

What We Crave—And Why It Still Matters

At the core of every marriage are two longings: to be cherished and to be respected. That hasn't changed since Eden.

Men, in general, tend to feel emotionally grounded when they sense respect—when their effort is acknowledged, their intentions aren't questioned, and their presence is valued. Women often draw strength from being deeply loved—not just with words, but through emotional connection, attentiveness, and shared vulnerability.

It's not that men don't need love or that women don't need respect. We all need both. But in many couples, what's *most deeply needed* is also what's *most easily withheld*.

When those needs go unmet, something shifts. He may shut down or act defensively. She might grow distant or emotionally cold. You find yourself stuck in a loop: pain leads to silence, silence leads to distance, and distance feeds more pain.

Dr. John Gottman, who has spent decades studying thousands of marriages, calls this the "negative sentiment override." In simple terms, once a relationship enters that space, even neutral comments get filtered through past hurt (Gottman and Silver 2015, 71). A spouse says, "Are you okay?" and the other hears, "You're a problem."

But here's what's beautiful: this cycle isn't permanent. There's a way out.

Heaven's Answer: Give What You'd Want to Receive

The apostle Paul, in Ephesians 5:33, didn't offer marriage advice based on opinion or culture. He gave divine direction:

"Let each one of you in particular so love his own wife as himself, and let the wife see that she respects her husband."

That's not a demand. It's a reflection of who God is. He doesn't love us because we're always lovable. He loves us because that's who He is. Likewise, respect and love in marriage aren't based on performance; they're based on covenant.

Ellen White put it beautifully when she said:

"Affection may be as clear as crystal and beauteous in its purity. ... Constantly behold Him, and your love for Him will daily become deeper and stronger" (*The Adventist Home*, 105).

But she didn't stop there. Affection grows only when we nurture it and tend to it like a flame that could go out if ignored. It's not automatic. It's cultivated.

When Science and Scripture Shake Hands

Modern psychology doesn't contradict Scripture—it often confirms it.

Dr. Sue Johnson, a renowned clinical psychologist, spent years researching what makes couples thrive. Her conclusion? Lasting connection isn't built on clever communication tricks. It's built on emotional safety. When people feel securely connected, they fight less and love more. When that bond feels threatened, even small arguments feel like war (Johnson 2019, 56).

Research on close relationships has shown that couples who regularly express appreciation and gratitude tend to experience higher relationship quality and satisfaction over time (Lambert et al. 2010, 574–580; Fincham and May 2020, 282–287).

On a broader scale, communities with more stable two-parent families tend to experience lower crime and fewer adverse childhood experiences, patterns that are linked in turn to better mental health outcomes for children and adolescents (Mangual, Wilcox, Cannon, and Price 2023). Marriage done well doesn't just bless the home—it blesses the neighborhood.

And ultimately, it blesses God. Because when we love each other well, we show the world what love from above really looks like.

As Ellen White said:

"Marriage, a union for life, is a symbol of the union between Christ and His church" (*Testimonies for the Church*, vol. 7, p. 46).

When two believers live out that kind of love, their home becomes a sermon. No pulpit needed.

Walking the Talk: Practical Steps to Real Harmony

1. Read the Word together.

Don't just do your morning devotions separately and call it good. Sit down together. Read slowly. Discuss what you hear God saying, and let Scripture form the rhythm of your relationship.

- Try starting with Ephesians 5 or 1 Corinthians 13.
- Talk about what each passage means to you. Go beyond what it says to how it applies to your life now.
- Share vulnerably. Scripture is more powerful when it shapes us both.

2. Get curious about each other.

The person you married isn't static. They're growing, changing, evolving—just like you.

3. Understand each other's world.

You shouldn't only talk about your hopes, worries, pressures, and joys when things are going wrong or when you have to make a big decision. Instead, these conversations should become a sacred rhythm in the relationship that lets each partner safely show new parts of their personality while being met with interest and kindness. Gottman and Silver assert, "Emotionally intelligent couples are intimately familiar with each other's world" (2015, 48). This closeness needs to be built up through regular conversation and not taken for granted.

- Ask, "What's making you feel most loved lately?" or "What am I missing that you wish I'd see?"
- Learn each other's love languages again. And again.
- Listen to understand, not to fix.

4. Pray like you're building something eternal.

Pray alone for your spouse. Then pray together. Prayer isn't magic—it's intimacy. When you invite God into your marriage, He brings wisdom you don't have and healing you can't manufacture.

- Ask God for empathy. For insight. For softness.
- Pray for courage to apologize and humility to change.
- Pray that your love reflects His.

5. Be humble like Christ by serving others without expecting anything in return.

Humility isn't thinking less of yourself; it's thinking of yourself less. In marriage, this means looking for ways to help your spouse, even with small, everyday tasks.

- Put their needs first. Pay attention to what your spouse needs and help out without being asked. It could be making their favorite snack or taking care of a chore they dislike.

- When you hurt your spouse, say sorry honestly. And when they hurt you, try to forgive quickly instead of holding onto anger.
- Tell your spouse what you love about them or what they're good at. When they're having a tough time, be patient and offer to help instead of pointing out their mistakes.
- Lead and follow with love. Show your love by serving your spouse in simple ways every day. And trust them by listening and supporting their ideas, working together as a team.

You and your spouse can go from knowing God's plan for marriage to actually living it out by taking these four steps on a regular basis. It will take patience, grace, and a constant commitment to seek God's guidance together to get there.

Marriage is not a relationship that stays the same; it is a dynamic union that shows God's glory. It is like gardening in that you have to plant carefully, prune carefully, and keep an eye on it all the time.

Reflection and Assessment Guide

Key Scripture

> "And the LORD God said, 'It is not good that man should be alone; I will make him a helper comparable to him'" (Genesis 2:18).

Reflection Questions
(For individual use, such as journaling)

1. **Divine Intentionality**
   - In what ways does your view of marriage align with God's original design in Genesis 2?

- How do you see mutuality, equality, and purpose reflected in your current or future relationship?

2. Love and Respect

- Do you feel more naturally inclined to express **love** or **respect**? Why do you think that is?
- What does your spouse need more of from you?
- Reflect on a moment when you felt deeply **loved** or **respected**. What made that moment impactful?
- How can you create a rhythm of mutual care, appreciation, and understanding in your marriage?

3. The Negative Cycle

- Have you experienced the "negative cycle" in a relationship—where love or respect was lacking and caused conflict or distance?
- How can an awareness of this dynamic help you respond more graciously in the future?

4. Spiritual Perspective

- What does it mean to you that your marriage (or future marriage) is meant to reflect Christ's love for the church?
- How would viewing your spouse as a divine gift change your daily interactions?

Couple Conversation Starters

Take turns asking each other the following questions. Be honest, gentle, and open-hearted.

- What makes you feel most **respected** by me?
- What does **love** look like to you in our relationship—daily, emotionally, spiritually?
- What areas of our marriage could better reflect God's original blueprint?

- How can I be a better *ezer kenegdo*—a supportive, equal partner—in this season of our lives?

Marriage Assessment Checklist

Check the boxes that apply to your relationship today. Be honest, and use this as a growth tool.

Statement	✔
We study Scripture or pray together regularly.	
We openly discuss each other's emotional and spiritual needs.	
I feel respected and valued in our relationship.	
I intentionally express love to my spouse in their preferred "language."	
We actively work through disagreements without contempt or withdrawal.	
I see our marriage as a reflection of God's covenant love.	
We practice mutual submission and Christlike humility.	
I believe our relationship is aligned with God's sacred design.	

Reflection: What patterns do you notice? Which areas need intentional nurturing?

Practical Applications

- **Create a "Marriage Mission Statement"**: Write a short paragraph together that outlines your shared values, spiritual goals, and how you want your relationship to reflect God's design.

- **Start a Weekly Check-In Ritual:** Set a weekly time to ask each other two simple questions:

1. How can I show you love/respect this week?
2. How did I do this past week?

- **Meditate on Scripture:** Memorize or reflect on **Ephesians 5:33** this week: "Each one of you also must love his wife as he loves himself, and the wife must respect her husband."

Prayer Focus

"Let the words of my mouth and the meditation of my heart be acceptable in Your sight, O LORD, my strength and my Redeemer" (Psalm 19:14).

Spend time praying individually or together using this simple guide:

"Lord, thank You for designing marriage as a reflection of Your love. Help me to better understand and honor my spouse's unique needs. Teach us to live with humility, grace, and mutual respect. Align our hearts with Your original blueprint so that our love may glorify You and bless others. Amen."

Recommended Reading for Deeper Study

- *Love and Respect* by Dr. Emerson Eggerichs
- *Hold Me Tight* by Dr. Sue Johnson
- *The Ministry of Healing* by Ellen G. White (chapter 29: "The Builders of the Home")
- *The Seven Principles for Making Marriage Work* by Dr. John Gottman

Final Thoughts

One truth that lingers with quiet clarity is that respect is not a secondary need for a man—it is the air his heart breathes. When respect is absent, love struggles to be felt; when it is present, love finds room to flourish. In the pages ahead, we will explore how respect functions as the oxygen of a man's soul, and how a woman can learn to speak this language with strength, grace, and integrity—without silencing her voice, diminishing her worth, or compromising her authenticity. In God's design, respect is not submission of self, but a sacred offering that nurtures harmony, dignity, and enduring love within marriage.

━━━━━━━━━━ Prayer Focus ━━━━━━━━━━

"Father, sometimes we forget that You are the originator of marriage. Help us to recognize our spouse not as a source of frustration or habit, but as a precious gift You have carefully placed in my life." Please soften our heart where selfishness has crept in. Tear down the walls that pride has built. "Teach us how to walk together, steady, humble, and united, just like You wanted us to from the start."

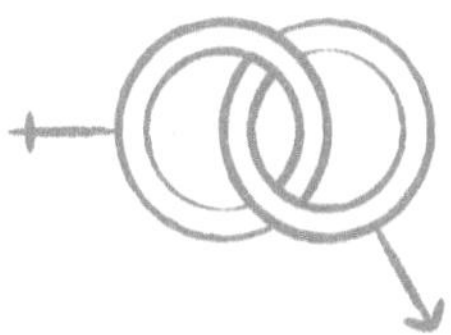

RESPECT—THE OXYGEN OF A MAN'S SOUL

"Let the wife see that she respects her husband." Ephesians 5:33b

Imagine waking up every morning with a spouse that believes in you, respects your leadership, listens without judgment, and expresses adoration even when they disagree. Many men see this as the pinnacle of a fulfilling relationship. Respect is more than a virtue for a man; it is the oxygen, emotional lifeline, and wellspring of all relational life. When men do not have it, they frequently experience emotional suffocation, disorientation, and disengagement.

This chapter explores the theology, sociology, and psychology of respect, with a focus on the male experience in marriage. It addresses both the biblical requirement and the scientific data showing that men prosper in circumstances where they are appreciated, notably by their wives. We will look at why men need respect and how women can learn to speak this language without losing their authenticity or value.

Understanding the Male Respect Reflex

For men, respect is akin to oxygen—it is an essential need that must be consistently met for them to feel valued, secure, and capable of thriving. Many couples, however, continue to struggle with how to demonstrate and receive respect, resulting in anger, resentment, and communication breakdowns.

1. Respect as a Sacred Trust, Not Subservience

In Ephesians 5:33, the apostle Paul, under divine inspiration, commands a wife to "respect her husband." This instruction, which is frequently misinterpreted as subservience or blind submission, is actually a call to actively affirm, honor, and exalt her husband in love. Respect here is about connection rather than control. It recognizes the husband's God-given dignity and responsibilities as spiritual head in the household while acknowledging the wife's equal worth and invaluable contribution.

Ellen White affirmed this dynamic by writing,

"The Lord has constituted the husband the head of the wife to be her protector; he is the house-band of the family, binding the members together, even as Christ is the head of the church and the Saviour of the mystical body" (*The Adventist Home*, 215).

This wonderful system is reciprocal rather than hierarchical in the traditional sense. It is not about masculine superiority. Instead, it is about mutually supplying what the other needs most deeply—respect for the man, love for the woman. These are not earned rewards but rather God-given responsibilities based on grace and supported by the Holy Spirit.

White also observed,

"The husband should let his wife know that he appreciates her work. The wife is to respect her husband. The husband is to love and cherish his wife; and as their marriage vow unites them as one, so their belief in Christ should make them one in Him" (*The Adventist Home*, 114).

In this relationship flow, a man flourishes when he believes his wife trusts him. When she genuinely expresses her appreciation for him—not as flattery, but as recognition of his efforts, ideals, and spiritual growth—it boosts his confidence and fires his desire to love her more completely. Respect is not only a gift, but also a significant investment in the emotional and spiritual atmosphere of the marriage.

2. The Practice of Respect: More than Silence or Flattery

Respect does not imply silence in the face of a mistake. The truth can be proclaimed in love (Ephesians 4:15), and correction can be given with respect. A wife respects her husband when she prays for him, speaks positively about him to others, attempts to understand his burdens, and includes him as a partner in the home's joint mission.

Interestingly, the apostle Paul's guidance in Ephesians predicted this dynamic, delivering timeless knowledge that is consistent with modern psychological understanding. According to Dr. Emerson Eggerichs's research in *Love and Respect* (2004), when men feel insulted, they frequently shut down or react aggressively, whereas when women feel unloved, they prefer to protest or pursue emotionally. This cycle can lead to conflict unless couples agree to offer each other what they need unconditionally.

At its core, biblical respect is about relational righteousness. It follows the divine pattern of mutual honor:

"Be devoted to one another in love. Honor one another above yourself" (Romans 12:10, NIV).

As Christ exemplified servant leadership and sacrificial love, so should husbands and couples demonstrate mutual respect and redemptive care. When this idea is used in the home, the marriage becomes a haven for spiritual growth and emotional protection.

3. Theological Foundations of Respect in Marriage

At the heart of Ephesians 5:33 is a significant theological revelation: God has structured the marriage connection to symbolize the mystery of Christ and the church. In this sacred analogy, the husband's affection reflects Christ's selfless love for His bride, and the wife's respect mirrors the church's reverence for Christ—not out of fear or inferiority, but out of deep love, admiration, and covenantal fidelity.

Respect is therefore a spiritual imperative, not just an interpersonal skill. It is a reaction to God's created order and redemptive purpose. In verse 21, Paul incorporated his instruction to women into a larger call to reciprocal submission:

"Submit to one another out of reverence for Christ" (NIV).

The Greek term for "submit" (*hupotassō*) denotes voluntary surrender based on love and confidence, as opposed to forced servitude.

The wife's respect is covenantal, meaning she selects it voluntarily in accordance with God's will and the paradigm of Christlike discipleship.

Respect is frequently associated in the Old Testament with the Hebrew word *kabod,* which means "weight" or "glory." To honor someone means to place a high value on them. This theological weight is determined by position and divine calling rather than accomplishment. Just as we honor God for who He is rather than what He accomplishes, spouses are also required to honor each other for the holy roles they play in the marriage bond.

A wife's respect for her husband confirms God's divine confidence in him. She asks him to rise to the level of his sacred duty—not by nagging or shaming, but by dignifying him—and her respect becomes prophetic, seeing not only who he is but who he is called to be in Christ.

4. Respect as a Transformational Act of Grace

The biblical model of marriage establishes a divine feedback loop: the more a husband loves sacrificially, the more a wife finds it natural to respect; the more a wife respects sincerely, the more a husband is empowered to love. This rhythm echoes the Trinity itself—distinct individuals, mutual deference, and loving unity.

This reciprocal pattern is not transactional but transformational. Dietrich Bonhoeffer, a theologian, noted in *Letters and Papers from Prison* that marriage is more than your love for each other. "It has a higher dignity and power, and God brings you together" (1997, 27). Respect is one of the tools that can be used on a regular basis to foster such unity.

Respect is fundamental to a man's spiritual identity and emotional management. Dr. John Gottman's research has shown that men are more likely than women to emotionally disengage when they feel mistreated, insulted, or undervalued. This detachment might jeopardize intimacy and spiritual connection. In contrast, when a man feels appreciated and trusted, his emotional vulnerability and spiritual leadership develop.

The idea of respect is brought out in 1 Peter 3:1, 2, where Peter exhorts ladies to win their husbands "without a word" by their conduct "accompanied by fear." This doesn't mean silence but signifies the persuasive power of a godly demeanor—respect that calls a man upward, not outward in defense.

> "We must have the Spirit of God, or we can never have harmony in the home. The wife, if she has the spirit of Christ, will be careful of her words; she will control her spirit, she will be submissive, and yet will not feel that she is a bondslave, but a companion to her husband" (*The Adventist Home*, 117, 118).

Ultimately, respect in marriage is not given only because a husband has earned it but because Christ commands it. It is an act of obedience, faith, and worship. The wife who respects her husband is not encouraging immaturity or sin but is submitting to a higher authority—God Himself—while trusting Him to do the transforming work in both hearts.

Respect, then, becomes an act of grace. It says, "I see you not only for who you are but for who God is making you to be." It is anchored in the gospel, which calls every believer—husband and wife alike—to live in love, humility, and dignity.

Sociological Insights: Respect and Gender Dynamics

Sociological research has demonstrated that men prosper in circumstances where their efforts are respected, their judgment is trusted, and their leadership is supported. Respect in this context entails validating a husband's aims, strengthening his sense of responsibility, and boosting his contribution to the family's well-being. This does not imply condoning wrongs but rather fostering a culture of honor where correction is wrapped in affirmation, not accusation.

This desire for respect stems in part from traditional gender conditioning. Boys are taught from a young age that their capacity to demand the respect of others is an important indicator of their worth. As boys mature into men, the need for respect becomes profoundly ingrained, influencing their conduct, emotional responses, and even their sense of self.

Contemporary sociologists have examined how gender roles impact the experience of respect in partnerships. Risman and Davis studied how the traditional sex roles in marriage are changing, but the emotional wiring molded by gender expectations still plays a crucial role. They observed that men are socially conditioned to consider respect as a marker of personal value and success—especially within intimate relationships (Risman and Davis 2013, 733–755).

This is especially true in societies where masculinity is related to leadership, provision, and problem-solving. When a wife expresses trust in her husband's decisions, abilities, and character—even in disagreement—it reinforces his sense of purpose and enhances the marriage relationship. Conversely, continuous criticism or sarcasm can deeply wound. A man who feels mistreated generally replies not by talking but by withdrawing, a reaction called stonewalling. Gottman's research suggests that 85% of stonewallers in marriage are men, who physiologically shut down when overwhelmed by perceived criticism or contempt (1999, 37).

According to Gottman, mutual respect is one of the strongest predictors of marital stability. His "Four Horsemen of the Apocalypse"—criticism, contempt, defensiveness, and stonewalling—are red flags that frequently lead to the loss of respect in a relationship. Contempt is particularly dangerous, and it frequently manifests when a wife unconsciously undermines her husband's competence, intelligence, or efforts.

While both men and women need respect, men typically interpret disrespect as rejection of their personhood. A 2020 study of emerging adult couples found that perceiving one's partner as responsive and validating was associated with greater relationship satisfaction, including for young men (Lachance-Grzela et al. 2020). Respect communicates value, trust, and honor—key components of masculine emotional health.

The Cycle of Disrespect

Many marital conflicts stem not from major moral failings but from repeated micro-signals of disrespect. These might include:

- Public correction or contradiction
- Dismissal of ideas or opinions
- Withholding appreciation or affirmation
- Comparing unfavorably to others
- Excessive nagging or fault-finding

While such behaviors may not be intentional, they accumulate. Over time, the husband may shut down emotionally, grow distant, or seek validation elsewhere. Ellen White warned of this danger,

> "Let not your married life be one of contention. If you do, you will both be unhappy. Be kind in speech and gentle in action, giving up your own wishes. Watch well your words, for they have a powerful influence for good or for ill" (*The Adventist Home*, 115).

The antidote? Intentional, verbalized, and consistent respect. This is not flattery—it is the honest acknowledgment of who he is and what he brings to the relationship.

Respect in Action: Practical Tools for Wives

- **Speak Life:** Affirm his strengths regularly. "I really admire the way you handled that situation."
- **Listen First:** Before correcting, seek to understand his logic. Ask, "Can you walk me through your thinking?"
- **Support His Role:** Acknowledge his efforts as a provider, protector, and partner.
- **Honor Him in Public:** Avoid correcting or mocking him in front of others. Praise him instead.
- **Pray with and for Him:** Respect grows when both hearts are aligned with God's.

These actions foster emotional safety and open the door to deeper connection. Respect is not a one-time deed; it's a daily disposition.

Final Thoughts

Respect is not about submission; it's about celebration. It's the sacred act of seeing your spouse as God sees him: valuable, capable, and worthy of honor. When a wife chooses to respect her husband—even when he falters—she mirrors Christ's grace. And in that grace, marriages grow strong.

As you embark on this adventure together, keep in mind that you are more than just cohabitants or colleagues. You are the co-creators of a sacred union. And that union thrives when the air is full of love and the atmosphere is rich in respect.

When a man feels respected, he breathes deeply; when a woman feels profoundly loved, she blooms. Respect is the nourishment that holds a man's identity together, while love—expressed via delicate words, considerate actions, and unshakable commitment—speaks most plainly to a woman's heart. If chapter 2 helped us grasp men's deep soul-need for respect, then chapter 3 will introduce us to the corresponding emotional lifeline for women: love. In that chapter, we will look at how love, anchored in Christ's example, becomes the sacred language that develops trust, emotional closeness, and a woman's feeling of value inside the covenant of marriage.

Reflection and Assessment Guide

Reflection Questions

- In what ways do you express respect to your husband? What actions or words might unintentionally communicate the opposite?
- How does your husband react when he feels respected? How does he respond when he feels dismissed?
- What specific strengths can you affirm in your husband this week?
- Are there times when you may have unintentionally disrespected or dismissed your partner's contributions or ideas?
- Consider a time when you supported your spouse's leadership, character, or effort. What influence did it have?
- How can you grow in showing more intentional and heartfelt respect?

Couple Conversation Starters

- What does "feeling respected" look like to each of us personally?
- Can we recall a time in our relationship when respect between us was at its strongest? What contributed to that?
- Are there any current habits or communication patterns that diminish our mutual respect?

- How can we create a home culture where respect is felt, seen, and expressed daily?

Assessment Tool: Measuring the Respect Factor

Rate each statement based on your current relationship experience, using the following scale:

1 (Rarely True), 2 (Sometimes True), 3 (Often True), 4 (Usually True), 5 (Always True)

Be honest—this is for reflection and growth, not judgment.

Statement	Rating (1–5)
I feel that my spouse believes in my abilities and judgment.	
My spouse acknowledges and affirms my contributions to the family.	
We speak to each other with kindness, even during conflict.	
My suggestions and opinions are valued and considered.	
My spouse avoids correcting or mocking me in front of others.	
I receive verbal encouragement or appreciation from my partner often.	
We discuss decisions with mutual respect for each other's input.	
I feel safe expressing vulnerability without fear of ridicule.	
My spouse speaks positively about me in public.	
Our disagreements are handled with civility and grace.	

Total Score: _____ / 50

Scoring Interpretation:

- 41–50: *Respect-Rich Relationship*—You're building a strong foundation. Celebrate and continue cultivating this strength!
- 31–40: *Healthy but Growing*—There is consistent respect, but intentional improvement can elevate your connection.
- 21–30: *Tension Warning Zone*—Consider identifying patterns that may be creating disrespectful dynamics and commit to change.
- 10–20: *Red Zone*—Respect may be eroding. Consider prayer, counseling, and open-hearted conversations as next steps.

═══ Prayer Focus ═══

"Lord, teach me how to honor and uplift my spouse. Help me to see them through Your eyes— with grace, admiration, and patience. Where I've failed, help me change. Where I've succeeded, help me remain faithful. Fill our home with the fragrance of mutual respect."

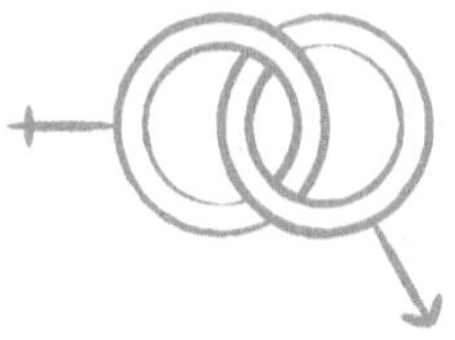

Chapter 3

LOVE—THE LANGUAGE OF A WOMAN'S HEART

"Husbands, love your wives, just as Christ also loved the church and gave Himself for her." Ephesians 5:25

If respect is the oxygen of a man's spirit, love is the lifeblood of a woman's universe. For many women, love is more than just an emotion; it is the environment (setting) she lives in. It is expressed in words, experienced in actions, and quantified in consistency. In this chapter, we look at how biblical love addresses psychological and emotional needs, confirming that a woman's innermost desire is to be recognized, respected, treasured, and pursued. Ellen White put it this way:

"True love is not a strong, fiery, impetuous passion. On the contrary, it is calm and deep in its nature. It looks beyond mere externals and is attracted by qualities alone. It is wise and discriminating, and its devotion is real and abiding" (*Letters to Young Lovers*, 31).

Love as Sacrificial Obedience

The apostle Paul gives husbands a wonderful example of love in Ephesians 5:25:

"Husbands, love your wives, just as Christ also loved the church and gave Himself for her."

Love, in the broadest biblical sense, is more than romance. It entails compassion, presence, sacrifice, and gentle care. This is not a casual recommendation or cultural adjustment; it is a heavenly command. Paul raises every husband's sight above human concepts of affection and romance, setting Christ Himself as an example. The Greek word for "love" in this text is *agapaō*, which also refers to God's unselfish and undeserved love for people. It is sacrificial, uncompromising, and redemptive; it is not a transactional relationship.

Jesus loved the church not because she was perfect, but because He wanted to perfect her. He loved with anticipation, unconditionality, and redemption. Humility (John 13:1–17), suffering (Isaiah 53:4, 5), and, lastly, His substitutionary death (Romans 5:8) demonstrated His love. When Paul instructs husbands to love "as Christ…loved the church and gave Himself for her," he places the cross at the heart of the marriage relationship. This is about more than just everyday acts of kindness, though such are important; it is about a willingness to sacrifice ego, pride, preferences, and personal comfort for the benefit of one's wife's well-being.

Ellen White affirmed the divine foundation of this love:

"Love is a precious gift, which we receive from Jesus. Pure and holy affection is not a feeling, but a principle" (*The Adventist Home*, 50).

Theological Dimensions of Christlike Love

Christ's love for the church is covenantal, meaning it is based on God's eternal promise and secured by His faithfulness. Similarly, a husband's love must be covenantal, not contractual. A contract states, "I will love you if..." A covenant states, "I will love you regardless."

The covenantal aspect of love is an expression of God's essence. The Bible compares God's relationship with His people to that of a faithful spouse and his occasionally unfaithful wife (as depicted in Hosea 2:19, 20 and Jeremiah 31:3). Christ came to redeem and cleanse the church, not because she deserved His love, but because His love is redeeming.

A husband does not withdraw affection when his wife does not satisfy his expectations. Instead, he embodies Christ's patience, tenderness, and perseverance. His leadership is cruciform, which means it resembles the cross, rather than being autocratic.

Christ's Love as Transformative Power

In Ephesians 5:26, 27, Paul explains that Christ's objective in loving the church was to sanctify and cleanse it so that it may be presented to Him as a magnificent church. Christ's love is not static; it is cleansing. Similarly, a husband's love should encourage growth, healing, and spiritual flourishing in his wife.

Ellen White reflected this ideal when she wrote,

"Let every step toward a marriage alliance be characterized by modesty, simplicity, sincerity, and an earnest purpose to please and honor God" (*The Adventist Home*, 49).

This transformational love fosters perfection rather than demanding it. It does not pass judgment but rather bestows blessings. It perceives potential and carefully harnesses it. As Christ prays for His bride, bears her burdens, and nourishes her soul, so must a husband devote himself to his wife's spiritual support.

Christ's Love and Servant Leadership

Jesus's leadership style revolved around service to others. In John 13, just before being crucified, Jesus washed the disciples' feet, as was customary for slaves to do. He then informed them,

> "I have given you an example, that you should do as I have done to you" (John 13:15).

Christian males should aim to exhibit this form of love. It does not demand compliance, but rather faith. It is not dominant, but rather dignified. It does not govern, but rather cultivates. Ellen White note

> "The marriage relation is holy, and it is to be entered into with a full sense of its responsibilities" (*Testimonies for the Church* 4, 504).

This sacred trust needs an ongoing reliance on Christ, the true source of this type of love. A man cannot develop agape love on his own. He must receive it before he can offer it.

Gender, Love, and Social Expectations

According to sociology, women are usually taught to value marital harmony, emotional depth, and nurture. According to Risman and Davis (2013, 733–755), even when gender roles shift, women continue to internalize the belief that love must be spoken and demonstrated as opposed to implied.

This socialization sets expectations in marriage: women want to hear "I love you," but they also want to "see" it—in tone of voice, warmth of touch, presence in stressful moments, and effort put into shared responsibilities.

Gottman discovered that little gestures—a kiss goodbye, a text during the day, or an extended hand during a walk—create what he refers to as "emotional bids." When spouses respond to these bids, marital connection flourishes. When they ignore or reject them, emotional alienation occurs (Ury 2024).

The Need to Be Loved: A Woman's Emotional Framework

Gottman's research summarizes predictors of relationship satisfaction and emotional responsiveness in couples, especially women's satisfaction. (See "Marriage and Couples – Research," The Gottman Institute, 2025, and "What Do Women Really Want?" The Gottman Institute, 2016.)

Psychological research has found that women frequently sense love through emotional availability, affectionate communication, acts of kindness, and continuous fulfillment of commitments. Neglect, inattention, or emotional retreat are frequently viewed as rejection instead of distance. Research on perceived partner responsiveness shows that when women experience their partners as emotionally responsive and attentive, they feel more loved, valued, and secure in the relationship (Reis et al. 2004; Reis 2013; Eri et al. 2024).

Love with Skin On: Practical Ways to Show Love

- **Expressive Words:** Regularly say "I love you," and be specific about what you love.

- **Time Together:** Prioritize free time to speak, laugh, and connect.
- **Physical Touch:** Non-sexual touch, such as hand-holding, hugs, and kisses, promotes emotional intimacy.
- **Acts of Service:** Assisting with chores, errands, or daily pressures speaks volumes.
- **Listening with Empathy:** Hear her out without offering solutions; only offer advice when solicited.
- **Faithful Presence:** Show up emotionally as well as physically. Be present with your mind, heart, and soul.

These expressions reassure a woman that she is appreciated, not just tolerated; valued, not just needed.

Barriers to Love: Why Women Withdraw

When love is lacking, inconsistent, or conditional, many women tend to emotionally withdraw. Symptoms may include:

- Withholding affection
- Growing critical or distant
- Overfunctioning in family roles to compensate
- Seeking emotional fulfillment elsewhere (e.g., children, work, friends)

Ellen White warned,

"In many cases it is the lack of thoughtful attention, the manifestation of little acts of kindness, and gentle courtesy, that makes the wives hearts sad, and makes the home life so unhappy" (*The Adventist Home*, 335).

Love is not a luxury in marriage; it is the primary fuel for feminine development. When a wife feels valued and appreciated, she provides generously, builds continuously, and nourishes tirelessly.

Final Thoughts

Love is forged, not discovered. It is not a spark of emotion; it is a fire that must be fed. When a husband decides to love his wife with Christlike dedication, he builds the groundwork for domestic security, tenderness, and joy. And as she blooms under that love, the entire family benefits from it.

Love is the language of a woman's heart. Learn, speak, and live it.

As we have seen, love is more than a feeling or a lyrical ideal; it is a sacred language that speaks deeply to a woman's heart. However, for this love to be genuinely transforming, it must transcend words and take concrete action. A wife feels loved not just when she hears it, but also when she sees it in daily actions of kindness, compassion, and attentiveness. In the following chapter, we will look at how love becomes nurturing—how a husband can support his wife's emotional, spiritual, and relational needs in ways that recognize her dignity and foster trust. We will go from recognizing her desire for love to finding practical, Christ-centered methods to communicate that love in the ordinary moments that help a marriage thrive.

Reflection and Assessment Guide

Reflection Questions
- How do you define love in the context of your marriage?
- Have you been emotionally available to your spouse lately? If not, what has stood in the way?
- What are three ways you've expressed love to your partner in the past week?

- Are there any instances where you were physically present yet emotionally distant?
- Are there any emotional bids from your spouse that you may have ignored or dismissed?
- What does your wife do when she feels emotionally connected?
- How can you become more consistent in expressing love—verbally, physically, and emotionally?

Couple Conversation Starters

- What specific behaviors or words make each of us feel most loved?
- Do we feel emotionally connected during daily routines or only in major events?
- How do we handle emotional disconnection when it happens?
- How can we become more emotionally available to one another?
- What new habit could we adopt to strengthen emotional intimacy in our relationship?

Assessment Tool: The Love Connection Index

Rate each statement based on your current relationship experience, using the following scale:

1 (Rarely True), 2 (Sometimes True), 3 (Often True), 4 (Usually True), 5 (Always True)

Statement	Rating (1–5)
My spouse makes time to talk and really listen to me.	
I feel emotionally connected and supported by my partner.	
My partner often uses affectionate words like "I love you."	
My partner regularly shows kindness and consideration toward me.	
I feel emotionally safe and free to express myself honestly.	
My partner is present and attentive, especially during stressful times.	
We share regular non-sexual physical affection (e.g., hugs, hand-holding).	
My spouse responds positively to my emotional needs or "bids" for connection.	
I feel cherished, pursued, and appreciated by my partner.	
Our home feels emotionally warm, affirming, and nurturing.	

Total Score: _______ / 50

Scoring Interpretation:

- 41–50: *Flourishing Love*—Your relationship thrives on emotional closeness and consistent acts of love. Keep nurturing it!

- 31–40: *Healthy but Room to Grow*—You have a good foundation, but being more intentional can take your connection deeper.

- 21–30: *Warning Zone*—Emotional intimacy may be lacking.

Open conversations and intentional love practices are needed.

- 10–20: *Critical Zone*—Emotional disconnection is a major issue. Consider seeking support, prayer, and professional guidance.

Prayer Focus

"Lord, teach me how to love deeply, speak kindly, and act patiently. Help me to create a safe emotional space where my spouse feels seen, heard, and cherished. May our love reflect Your tender heart and constant presence."

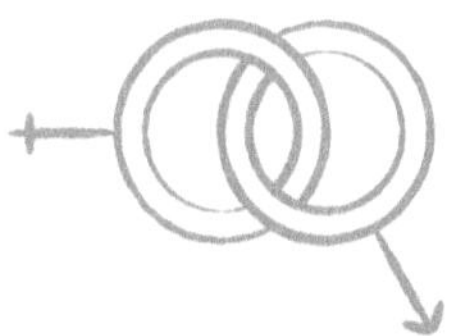

Chapter 4:

LOVE THAT NURTURES—MEETING HER NEEDS

"Husbands, love your wives, just as Christ also loved the church and gave Himself for her." Ephesians 5:25

A woman's heart is like a plant that requires care. Her greatest desire in a marriage is to feel deeply, safely, and unconditionally loved, even though she is strong, intelligent, and competent. God designed this emotional need, and it is not a sign of weakness. A woman thrives in the soil of love, just as a man gains strength from respect.

As we've already seen in Ephesians 5:25, the apostle Paul, under divine inspiration, issues a clear mandate:

"Husbands, love your wives, just as Christ loved the church and gave himself up for her."

This is not a passive relationship. It is active, selfless, attentive, and consistent. It is the type of love that analyzes the beloved, anticipates her needs, and looks after her well-being.

Love That Listens

Listening is more than just a communication skill in the complex web of relationships, particularly the sacred bond of marriage. It is a holy act of love. It is relatively common for women to live in emotional silence, not because their husbands say nothing, but because their husbands do not actually hear them. Listening, in its purest form, is a deeply spiritual relationship with another's soul. It involves tuning one's heart to another's voice, acknowledging feelings, and validating experiences—even those that are painful or unsaid.

Scripture teaches us how important listening is to God.

"Let every person be quick to hear, slow to speak, and slow to anger" (James 1:19, ESV).

This wisdom serves as a reminder that in order to love well, we must listen well. A husband who listens not only receives words but also his wife. He respects her inner world, unspoken prayers, and silent burdens.

Jesus Christ demonstrated this with divine perfection. When Jesus met the Samaritan woman at the well (John 4:1–26), He did not interrupt, correct, or diminish her pain. Instead, He drew out her story and listened with sympathetic intent. His involvement offered healing, dignity, and salvation to a marginalized lady in society. And later, when another woman, Mary, sat at Jesus's feet, He declared,

"Mary has chosen the better part" (Luke 10:42, CEB).

He validated her desire to be heard and spiritually nurtured, in contrast to a culture that stifled women's voices.

These episodes in Christ's ministry are not coincidental; they are instructional. Husbands are to follow in His footsteps.

"Husbands, love your wives as Christ loved the church and gave Himself for her" (Ephesians 5:25).

Listening with focus, empathy, and patience is part of sacrificial love. When a man listens to his wife, he provides a safe haven in which she feels emotionally secure, known, and loved. This encourages intimacy and reciprocal trust and creates an environment in which both partners can grow emotionally and spiritually.

Listening is the key to understanding. According to Proverbs 20:5,

"The purposes of a person's heart are deep waters, but one who has insight draws them out" (NIV).

When a husband listens intently, he becomes the wise man who softly uncovers the treasures of his wife's heart.

Love That Covers and Protects

Married love is defined by protection and honor. In one of the most well-known passages on love, the apostle Paul states that love "always protects, always trusts, always hopes, [and] always perseveres" (1 Corinthians 13:7, NIV). True love, then, is more than just patience and kindness; it is a shield. It protects against injury, whether physical, mental, or spiritual.

The biblical ideal of marriage places a strong emphasis on a husband's protective function. He is not expected to control or oppress his wife but to protect her with grace, compassion, and support.

"You are a hiding place for me; you preserve me from trouble; you surround me with shouts of deliverance" (Psalm 32:7, ESV).

Just as God protects us in His love, a husband is responsible for creating a sanctuary of calm and safety for his wife.

This protective love is not about control; it is a sign of authentic respect. It includes safeguarding her reputation, acknowledging her weaknesses, and promoting her goals. According to Proverbs 31:11, 12,

"The heart of her husband safely trusts her. ... She does him good, and not evil, all the days of her life."

A loving spouse trusts and respects his wife in such a way that she thrives in his care.

Again, Jesus is the best example. He never used his position of authority to bully or manipulate others. Instead, He gave His life for those He loves, empowered the weak, and advocated for the oppressed (John 10:11). In marriage, a husband is expected to embody the same type of servant-hearted, protective love—one that shields, uplifts, and nurtures.

When a man defends his wife against the harshness of the world and preserves her dignity in all conversations and decisions, he reflects God's covenantal heart. Ephesians 5:28 states,

"In the same way husbands should love their wives as their own bodies. He who loves his wife loves himself" (ESV).

Love That Reflects Christ

Together, love that listens and love that protects provide a powerful and Christ-centered vision of marriage. They are not distinct virtues but two manifestations of the same divine love. Listening promotes emotional safety. Protection promotes spiritual security. Both enable love to expand, develop, and withstand life's obstacles.

When husbands choose to listen with empathy and protect with integrity, they reflect the heart of Christ. They not only bless their wives but also reinforce their marriage's foundation. Such love—humble, sacred, and healing—is uncommon in our world. However, when practiced, it demonstrates the gospel's transformative power in everyday life.

> "Love is the basis of godliness. Whatever the profession, no man has pure love to God unless he has unselfish love for his brother. But we can never come into possession of this spirit by *trying* to love others. What is needed is the love of Christ in the heart" (*Christ's Object Lessons*, 384).

Love That Pursues

In the early stages of a relationship, love frequently comes naturally. There are dates, flowers, phone calls, and heartfelt messages. However, as time passes and life's obligations grow, intentionality must take precedence over spontaneity. Pursuing your bride does not stop at the altar. In many ways, it starts there.

Psychological research validates emotional connection. Dr. Sue Johnson, the creator of Emotionally Focused Therapy, argues that a secure emotional bond is the central factor in thriving intimate relationships. She notes that many women are especially sensitive to emotional cues in the relationship and look for ongoing signals of affection and emotional attunement as a source of security (Johnson 2008).

Women experience a profound sense of love when their husbands acknowledge and appreciate their subtle gestures of care. This includes attentively listening to their daily experiences without offering immediate solutions to their concerns, remembering the matters that hold significance for them, and making dedicated time for meaningful connections, even amidst demanding schedules.

A woman's emotional security is contingent upon a man's emotional availability, in addition to his physical presence. Ellen White advocated for husbands to exhibit patience, thoughtfulness, tenderness, and attentiveness towards their wives and to consistently strive to engender joy and contentment within the household. She underscored the significance of mutual kindness, patience, and endeavors to cultivate happiness within the marital bond (*The Adventist Home*, 112).

According to Gottman's research, the husband's ability to attune to and respond to his wife's emotional bids is the most important factor influencing her contentment in a relationship. Wives must trust that their husbands will guard their hearts. This includes staying away from criticism, sarcasm, shame, and dismissal, especially when speaking in public. It requires creating a safe space where she can freely express her emotions, whether it's crying, failing, or feeling terrified. "Active listening will keep conversations calm and allow you and your partner to make progress in the conversation" (Panganiban 2025).

Spiritual leadership is another aspect of protective love. When a wife's husband prays for her, initiates family worship, and demonstrates integrity, she feels safe. He becomes her priest, standing between her and the chaos of the world.

Love That Serves

Christ loved the church by laying down His life. He stooped low to wash feet, carry burdens, and bear sins. Similarly, a husband demonstrates love through service. Doing the dishes, assisting with the children, listening during exhaustion, or sacrificing personal comfort—these are acts of Christlike love.

Service is never about winning favor; rather, it is about reflecting the character of Jesus. In serving his wife, a husband nurtures not only her happiness but also her sense of worth. She feels seen. She feels valued. She feels cherished.

According to social researcher Shaunti Feldhahn, women in her studies reported that small, daily expressions of thoughtfulness and modest demonstrations of care often have a greater impact on relationships than occasional, spectacular gestures (Feldhahn 2013, 36).

Love in Seasons of Conflict

No marriage is free from conflict, and in those moments love must hold steady. During conflict, a woman's need for love often rises, even as her sense of being loved may decline. She desires reassurance and connection most at the very moment when the tension makes it hardest to feel understood. This is why gentle love in conflict becomes a powerful act of grace. When her husband maintains a compassionate tone, kind body language, and firm commitment, he reassures her of their emotional safety. This does not imply avoiding difficult realities or concealing emotions. It means communicating in ways that value the relationship over being correct. Love sees disagreement as an opportunity for better understanding as opposed to an opportunity for war.

From a psychological standpoint, emotional regulation is critical to conflict resolution. Bloch, Haase, and Levenson (2014, 130) found that wives' downregulation of negative emotions and behaviors during marital conflict predicts greater satisfaction for both partners over time, mediated by constructive communication like mutual negotiation and expressions.

Final Thoughts

Many women carry wounds from past neglect, abuse, or rejection. In marriage, love can become a healing balm. A husband's consistent attention and emotional involvement can restore confidence, rebuild trust, and awaken joy. True love transforms. It brings out beauty, power, and calm. It develops a woman's ability to love in return, give of herself completely, and trust sincerely. God has endowed husbands with a special responsibility to reflect His love to their wives. When a wife feels cherished, she becomes more radiant, more expressive, and more whole. Her femininity flourishes, and her home becomes a haven.

Love does not require a huge gesture once a year. It is a daily decision, a tone of voice, a hug, a shared burden, a silent prayer. It is an echo of God's words in Jeremiah 31:3,

"I have loved you with an everlasting love."

In the divine dance of marriage, let love lead.

This chapter has delved into the profound emotional and spiritual need of a wife to experience love in tangible, consistent, and emotionally resonant forms.

When a husband learns to communicate in the language of nurturing love, his wife experiences a profound sense of safety, value, and happiness. Love, expressed not only through words but also through consistent acts of care, creates a nurturing environment that facilitates her development. Conversely, just as a woman's soul blossoms with love, a man's spirit can flourish under genuine respect. To attain divine harmony, both partners must identify and respond to each other's underlying emotional needs. As we proceed into chapter 5, we will explore how respect can heal past hurts, affirm a man's identity, and draw him closer to his wife's heart and God's heart.

Reflection and Assessment Guide

Key Scriptures

> "Husbands, love your wives, just as Christ loved the church and gave himself up for her" (Ephesians 5:25, NIV).

> "Love is patient, love is kind. … It always protects, always trusts, always hopes, always perseveres" (1 Corinthians 13:4–7, NIV).

> "Husbands, love your wives and do not be harsh with them" (Colossians 3:19, NIV).

Ellen G. White Insight

> "Husbands should be careful, attentive, constant, faithful, and compassionate. They should manifest love and sympathy. … He will seek to keep his wife in health and courage. He will strive to speak words of comfort, to create an atmosphere of peace in the home circle" (*Adventist Home*, 228).

Reflection Questions

- What does "feeling loved" mean for your wife (or women in general)?
- What aspects of your current understanding of marital love does Christ's example of selfless love call into question?
- In what ways might your love be uneven, distracted, or misunderstood?
- Which of your wife's needs (emotional, spiritual, or bodily) are most frequently overlooked—and why?
- How do you show love during stress, conflict, or personal struggle?
- What tangible acts of love do you believe your wife would appreciate today?
- How can you improve your ability to provide nurturing love even when it is inconvenient or not reciprocated?

Practical Applications

Daily Practice	Description
Emotional Check-In	Ask your wife daily, "How is your heart today?" Listen without fixing—just be present.
Acts of Service	Without being asked, do one small task that lightens her load each day.
Words of Affirmation	Speak a loving word each day about who she is, not simply what she does. For example, "You're wise," "You inspire me," or "I love your compassion."
Touches of Love	Offer affectionate, non-sexual touch regularly, such as hugs, hand-holding, or kisses on the forehead.
Spiritual Leadership	Pray over her, with her, and for her on a consistent basis. Create moments of shared spiritual reflection.

Couples Activity: The Love Inventory

Goal: Identify and affirm each other's love languages and emotional needs.

Steps:
1. Each spouse responds to the question, "When do you feel most loved by me?"
2. Exchange responses and explain what each love expression means to you.
3. Commit to using one of your spouse's primary love expressions every day this week.
4. Wrap up the activity by holding hands and praying for your marriage.

Discussion Prompts

- Why do you believe women commonly associate love with emotional connection and security?
- How has media, culture, or upbringing influenced the way you express or accept love?
- What are the most prevalent obstacles to men constantly expressing love?
- How can biblical love be exercised when emotions are absent?
- How does sacrificial love mend a wounded or distant marriage?

Self-Assessment Tool for Husbands

Rate yourself on the following statements, using the following scale:

1 (Rarely True), 2 (Sometimes True), 3 (Often True), 4 (Usually True), 5 (Always True)

Statement	1	2	3	4	5
I express love in ways my wife understands and values.					
I spend intentional, uninterrupted time with my wife regularly.					
I speak words of kindness and affection daily.					
I show care for her emotions and listen with empathy.					
I lead in prayer and model spiritual love.					

Reflection: What area needs your attention this week? What can you do today to increase your wife's sense of being deeply loved?

Prayer Focus

"Lord, help me to love my wife with the same sacrificial love You've shown to me. Teach me to notice her needs, cherish her heart, and lead with gentleness and humility. May my love be a sanctuary for her soul, a testimony of Your grace, and a reflection of the gospel in our home. In Jesus' name, amen."

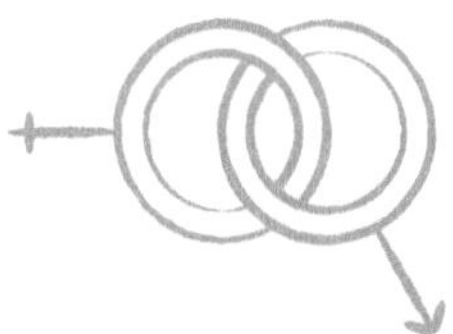

RESPECT THAT HEALS—MEETING HIS NEEDS

"Nevertheless, let each one of you in particular so love his own wife as himself, and let the wife see that she respects her husband." Ephesians 5:33

He sat across from me, softly crying. It was something he had never done in front of anyone, let alone his wife. He shared, "All I want is for her to believe in me. I work very hard at work. I strive to take charge. But I never feel good enough, no matter what I succeed in."

His wife was undoubtedly in love with him. But she had no idea that her constant corrections, scathing remarks, and emotional detachment were destroying his soul. She didn't mean to harm anyone. She was trying to be honest, share her concerns, and make things better. But to him it sounded like criticism. And to a man's emotions, constant criticism comes across as contempt.

This chapter explores how biblical respect is not a mindless act of submission but rather a firm Christlike position that builds intimacy in a man's heart, rebuilds trust, and instills confidence.

What Respect Means to a Man

The idea of respect in marriage has been misinterpreted and even denigrated by many women. Some assume that respect means keeping quiet or simply doing whatever one is told. Scripture paints a different picture entirely. Respect is all about honor, not power. It is about appreciating the gravity of a man's vocation, the breadth of his load, and the earnestness of his endeavors—even when they are unsuccessful.

A man of integrity is not a perfect person. He is a man whose existence is acknowledged, whose voice is important, and whose dignity is valued. Respect says, "I have faith in your leadership," particularly when things are tough. "I notice your efforts," it acknowledges while progress is slow. Even though he is still changing, it says, "I have faith in the person God intends you to become."

Respecting His God-Given Identity

Paul's advice in Ephesians 5:33, "and the wife must respect her husband" (NIV), is a holy requirement derived from divine design rather than an antiquated cultural tradition. A woman's deliberate decision to respect God's creative order and redemptive calling on her husband's life, not a man's flawlessness, is what earns respect.

Ephesians 5:33 uses the Greek term *phobeō*, which means to treat with dignity, reverence, or deference. It suggests a sacred reverence, not terror, for the husband's God-given role in the marriage covenant in this context. Wives are asked to revere just as husbands are invited to love sacrificially like Christ (Ephesians 5:25)—not because the man is always deserving but because Christ is.

Respect is the lifeblood of a man; it is more than just being kind. Paul does not imply respect as a cultural courtesy in

Ephesians 5:33; rather, he demands it as part of God's purpose for marital harmony and restoration. Respect ministers to the essence of a husband's identity, just as love attends to the deepest emotional needs of a wife. Even in tiny ways, a woman can help her husband heal when she makes the decision to respect, affirm, and trust him.

Respecting a husband means seeing him as a partner in grace, a leader-in-training, and a son of God. It is a means to resist the subtle societal deterioration of biblical manhood and conform to the blueprint of heaven. Respect can also be a prophetic act of faith, even in the face of a husband's problems, acknowledging not just who he is but also who, by God's grace, he is becoming.

"And the Lord God said, 'It is not good that man should be alone; I will make him a helper comparable to him'" (Genesis 2:18).

God created the woman to be a strong complement to man, not a rival or an evaluator. Consequently, respect transforms into a spiritual ministry that elevates, empowers, and sustains the husband's aspiration to lead with humility rather than aggressiveness.

With sensitivity and visionary clarity, Ellen White cautioned against an attitude of dominance or criticism within the family. She underscored that wives should refrain from attempting to dominate their husbands and instead should respect their judgment and leadership in the household (*The Adventist Home,* 114, 115).

The Wounds of Disrespect

Respect is like balm for a man's soul. A husband is able to love more passionately, serve more faithfully, and lead more responsibly when he feels valued. However, disrespect often takes the form of dismissiveness and does not always show up as open contempt. This includes:

- Eye-rolling during a disagreement
- Interrupting him mid-sentence
- Making jokes at his expense in public
- Comparing him to other men ("Why can't you be more like...?")
- Giving the cold shoulder or silent treatment
- Undermining his decisions at home or in parenting
- Seizing leadership roles out of frustration ("I'll just do it myself—he'll mess it up anyway.")

These behaviors not only undermine intimacy and mutual trust, but they also hurt the male heart. Unhealed emotional wounds have the potential to harden a man's character over time, resulting in stubbornness, bitterness, or isolation. Maintaining a polite tone and position can influence the outcome of events. Even seemingly insignificant actions can serve as reminders of Proverbs 14:1, which states,

"The wise woman builds her house, but with her own hands the foolish one tears hers down" (NIV).

Furthermore, while these wounds may not manifest as evident bruises on the skin, they inflict profound emotional trauma. Men who feel mistreated are more prone to retreating. Some may exhibit passivity, lack of motivation, or even rage. Others may focus on their tasks, while still others may withdraw into silence. Others may seek external validation—not as an act of rebellion, but out of a sense of a void.

"A soft answer turns away wrath, but a harsh word stirs up anger" (Proverbs 15:1).

Respect as a Reflection of Christ

Respecting a husband is more than just elevating him; it reflects the character of Christ, who exemplified submission without loss of dignity. In Philippians 2:3–5, Paul encourages believers to prioritize others before themselves and approach relationships with humility and service:

"Do nothing from selfish ambition or conceit, but in humility count others more significant than yourselves. … Have this mind among yourselves, which is yours in Christ Jesus" (ESV).

In the marriage covenant, love and respect are reciprocal. A wife's respect is not won by perfection, but rather she gives it out of Christlike love. In doing so, she contributes to the redemption of her house. Respect fosters a climate in which love may blossom, conflict can be resolved, and leadership can develop.

Living the Theology of Respect

Respect does not imply blind agreement. Nor does it imply condoning sin or suppressing your voice. It means choosing to honor the man God is shaping. It is all about the tone of voice, the moment, faith, and the spiritual posture of your heart.

Peter also urges us,

"Wives, in the same way submit yourselves to your own husbands so that, if any of them do not believe the word, they may be won over without words by the behavior of their wives" (1 Peter 3:1, NIV).

This doesn't mean that respect is about remaining silent. It is about speaking with wisdom, clothed in gentleness and anchored in faith.

Respect in Action

So, what does healthy, healing respect look like?

1. **Speaking Words of Affirmation:** These are not flattering remarks. They are fuel.
   - "I'm proud of you."
   - "Thank you for working hard for us."
   - "I believe in your leadership."

2. **Trusting His Decisions:** Give him space to lead. Even if you would have handled the situation differently, trust his judgment, wherever feasible. Request his input. Invite his ideas. When a man believes his voice is important, he is more likely to take initiative.

3. **Listening Without Interrupting:** Allow him to express himself freely, without interrupting or finishing his thoughts. Treat him with the same amount of care and attention that you would expect while discussing your most intimate sentiments.

4. **Appreciating the Small Things:** Respect is more than just huge gestures; it is also about the simple things. Examples include "Thanks for checking out the car" or even "I really appreciate you helping out with the kids." These are the moments that make a difference.

5. **Defending Him Publicly:** Be careful of what you say about your husband in public and do not openly disparage or contradict him. If you disagree with him, talk to him privately. Remember that expressing respect in public preserves his dignity.

When Respect Is Hard: Loving Through Disappointment

There are times when respect seems impossible—when your husband has failed to lead adequately, made terrible judgments, or is emotionally distant. How do you show respect in these situations without being dishonest or enabling?

First, recognize that respect is not synonymous with approval. It is not about pretending he did not make mistakes. It is about choosing to continue treating him as someone formed in God's image, capable of redemption and growth. Respect states, "I disagree with what you did, but I still see the man God is shaping in you."

Second, communicate with courteous honesty. Rather than expressing, "You never listen to me," try, "I feel hurt when I do not feel heard." This moves the focus away from blaming and toward your feelings. Ask if the two of you can look into ways that can improve communication together. Using respectful, non-accusatory language protects his dignity while still addressing the issue.

Third, set boundaries without shame. Seek professional help if there have been significant breaches, such as emotional neglect, addiction, or infidelity. God never expects spouses to allow sin in the interest of submission. Love and respect must live alongside honesty and accountability.

Rebuilding Trust and Intimacy

Healing is possible in relationships that have broken down due to lack of respect. Begin with a prayer. Ask God to give you the sight to view your husband as He does. Look for what he is doing well and breathe life into those areas. Celebrate effort, not just results.

Practice "catching him" doing good. Thank him for the little things. Let him realize that his presence is important. And when you cultivate seeds of respect, do not be surprised if you start to reap the benefits of love. A respected man feels secure enough to love. A loved man develops the courage to lead.

Respect Motivated by the Fear of God

Ultimately, respect is not granted to an individual merely based on their merits or value in every situation. It is granted to them as an assignment from God, and your marriage represents your deep bond with Christ. Marriage, therefore, is not about matching your partner's behavior; it's about reflecting Christ's character in how you treat your partner.

Just as Christ loved us while we were still sinners, we can choose to honor even when it is difficult. That decision communicates loudly to a watching world. Your marriage becomes a living testimony of grace. When a wife speaks life, shows honor, and chooses to respect, she fosters an environment in which her husband can thrive emotionally, spiritually, and relationally. In doing so, she honors her covenant with God.

Marriage is not about being perfect; it is about discovering that sacred harmony. It is like a lovely dance, full of love and respect, freely given and happily received. It is a way of living honestly, for the glory of the one who made it all happen.

The biblical duty to honor one's spouse is unexpectedly pertinent in a world that frequently values independence above reliance on others. Ephesians 5:33 gives a heavenly template for a healthy relationship that goes beyond mutual respect. When a wife chooses respect, she improves not only her marriage but also her own self-esteem. Remember how damaging criticism is? Her words, however, also have the ability to transform everything and make things better. And if she has faith in her husband, he can become an excellent leader. A thousand lectures cannot match her peaceful trust in him. Finally, respect is not only his need; it is also her gift, and by giving it, she contributes to the building of a story of dignity, healing, and hope.

Final Thoughts

Respect isn't something you can learn; it's a way of being. When a man feels respected, he knows that people see him, trust him, and want him to be the best version of himself. Respect doesn't make differences go away or stop people from speaking up; it makes a safe space where people can grow without feeling ashamed. When you choose to respect someone, even when it's hard, you help God bring healing in your marriage, restore dignity, and build a love that lasts.

Reflection and Assessment Guide

Key Scriptures

"The wife must respect her husband" (Ephesians 5:33, NIV).

"They [husbands] may be won over without words by the behavior of their wives, when they see the purity and reverence of your lives" (1 Peter 3:1, 2, NIV).

"Outdo one another in showing honor" (Romans 12:10, ESV).

Ellen G. White Insight

Ellen White emphasized that the wife is to respect her husband, while the husband is to love and cherish his wife, uniting them as one in Christ (*The Adventist Home*, 114).

Reflection Questions

(Use these for personal journaling or a couple's discussion.)

- What does respect mean to you? How has your understanding of it changed after reading this chapter?
- What are three things your spouse does that you truly admire but may not have expressed appreciation for recently?
- Have you unintentionally disrespected your spouse in the past week? What did that look like?
- How do you respond when your husband tries to lead in an area where you feel more competent or experienced?
- What does it look like to offer "respectful honesty" in your relationship? Can you give an example from your experience?
- When is it hardest for you to show respect? How do you think God wants you to respond in those moments?
- How can your respect reflect your relationship with Christ—even when your spouse disappoints you?

Practical Applications

Daily Practice	Description
Speak Life	Begin each day with one affirming statement of your husband—text it, say it, or write it on a sticky note.
Honor in Public	Intentionally speak positively about your husband in front of others this week.
Prayer for Respect	Each morning, pray, "Lord, help me see my husband through Your eyes. Teach me to honor him even when it's hard."
Respect Journal	Start a journal with a list of ways your husband provides, protects, leads, or sacrifices for the family. Add to it daily. Share an entry with him once a week.

Couples Activity: Respect & Reconnect Evening

Goal: Rebuild emotional connection through honor and attentiveness.

Steps:

1. Set aside an evening with no phones or distractions.
2. Each partner writes down five things they respect about the other.
3. Exchange your lists and read them aloud to each other.
4. End the evening with prayer, thanking God for each other and asking for His help to grow in love and respect.

Discussion Prompts

- Why do you think respect is such a vital emotional need for men, based on the biblical and psychological insights in this chapter?
- In your culture, how is male leadership viewed? How does that influence the way women express respect?
- What are the dangers of offering respect only when a husband "deserves" it? How can we balance grace with accountability?
- How do healthy boundaries and respect work together in a Christian marriage?

Self-Assessment Tool for Wives

Rate yourself on the following statements, using the following scale:

1 (Rarely True), 2 (Sometimes True), 3 (Often True), 4 (Usually True), 5 (Always True)

Statement	1	2	3	4	5
I express gratitude for my husband's efforts regularly.					
I listen to my husband without interrupting or correcting.					
I trust his judgment and leadership, even when I disagree.					
I avoid sarcasm, criticism, or public shaming.					
I pray for and affirm his role as a husband and leader.					

Reflection: What areas do you feel strong in? Where would you like to grow?

Prayer Focus

"Heavenly Father, thank You for the gift of marriage. Teach me to honor my husband the way You honor Your children—with grace, truth, and strength. Help me to speak life and build him up. Let our marriage reflect Your love to the world. In Jesus' name, amen."

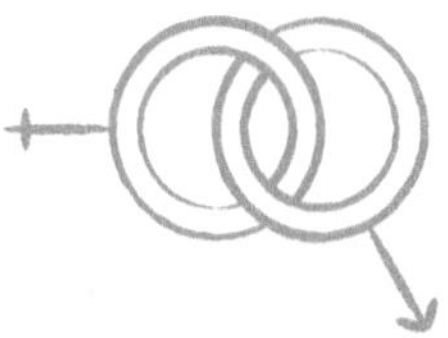

Chapter 6:

COMMUNICATION POWER—THE CONNECTIVE LANGUAGE

"A word fitly spoken is like apples of gold in a setting of silver." Proverbs 25:11

Communication is essential to the functioning of any relationship, but in a marriage, it becomes the sacred medium through which love and respect are shared. It is more than a simple verbal interaction; it is a soul connection. In periods of peace or conflict, communication between partners either deepens their intimacy or promotes emotional distance. This chapter looks at how communication can be transformed into a language of connection, a way to show love and respect for your spouse and God.

Gentle Responses: A Theology

One of the eternal lessons found in the Bible is that "a gentle answer turns away wrath, but a harsh word stirs up anger" (Proverbs 15:1). This is a theological fact based on the character of God Himself, not just a communication tip. God does not humiliate us into repentance; rather, He entices us with tenderness, as we witness throughout Scripture (Romans 2:4). Similar to this, marriage is supposed to be a haven where Christlike communication reflects the kindness of the Savior rather than a battlefield of acrimonious words and erratic emotions.

Being gentle is a form of controlled strength, not weakness. One of the fruits of the Spirit in fact (Galatians 5:22–23), gentleness is particularly necessary when tensions are high. To speak gently is to do it with grace, kindness, and self-control rather than to deny the truth or silence our voice. According to the Bible, every word we use has the potential to either strengthen or weaken our bonds with others. Proverbs 18:21 states that the tongue has the capacity to decide life or death.

Even in stressful situations, Jesus exemplified this heavenly tenderness. He refrained from retaliating when wrongfully accused (1 Peter 2:23). He responded with dignity and empathy when the adulterous woman was brought before Him (John 8:10, 11). His responses restored dignity and defused tensions, providing us with a model for emotional control and empathetic communication in our homes.

"Let your conversation be always full of grace, seasoned with salt, so that you may know how to answer everyone" (Colossians 4:6, NIV).

A gentle reaction is an accurate representation of the gospel; it conveys the message that patience is more persuasive than pressure and that love is stronger than anger. Couples who make a commitment to reacting tactfully, particularly when they are angry, are reflecting the very nature of Christ, who came to earth to redeem rather than to condemn.

"Be completely humble and gentle; be patient, bearing with one another in love" (Ephesians 4:2, NIV).

Therefore, being gentle in speech is more than just a matter of tone; it is a journey toward peace, a spiritual discipline, and a fruit of surrender. In a marriage where communication is frequent and emotions are intense, putting this biblical gentleness into practice turns uncomfortable situations into chances for grace, and disagreement into communion.

During the COVID-19 pandemic, a lot of couples had to deal with this difficulty like never before. They were confined to common areas and deprived of the diversions of employment or travel, compelling them to communicate constantly. However, many found that more time did not necessarily translate into greater understanding. According to the American Psychological Association (2020, 2), COVID-19 lockdown stress led nearly half of adults to report behaviors like snapping angrily (20%) or yelling at loved ones (17%), thus straining relationships.

The Sacred Art of Listening

One of the best ways to show love is to listen to others. Reading the heart is more important than simply hearing words. The very character of Christ, who never hurried people, disregarded their emotions, or interrupted their suffering, is reflected in active, compassionate listening.

According to Ellen White,

"If the will of God is fulfilled, the husband and wife will respect each other and cultivate love and confidence. Anything that would mar the peace and unity of the family should be firmly repressed, and kindness and love should be cherished" (*The Adventist Home*, 120).

This emphasizes the importance of sacred attentiveness.

According to psychologist Carl Rogers, when people are listened to with nonjudgmental, accepting attention, they often feel deep relief and begin to see previously overwhelming problems in a new, more hopeful light (1980, 126, 127). "You matter to me" is communicated in a marriage when someone listens with empathy rather than condemnation or solutions.

The sacred art of listening involves:

- Putting away your distractions and giving your whole attention
- Emotional mirroring—"It sounds like you are feeling..."
- Not assuming purpose, but instead, posing questions that show interest
- Acknowledging feelings before providing feedback

Love and respect can only thrive when there is emotional safety created through listening.

Fighting Fair and Resolving with Grace

Although disagreements are unavoidable, how a couple handles their disagreements determines whether the conflict is beneficial or destructive. According to Dr. John Gottman's research, couples who remain together handle conflict effectively by making "repair attempts"—minimum attempts to defuse tense situations, such as displaying vulnerability or utilizing comedy (2015, 85, 86).

To fight fairly:

- Focus on the issue rather than the individual.
- Instead of saying "You never listen," use "I" phrases like "I feel unheard."

- Establish ground rules for disagreements, such as no name-calling, shouting, or interrupting.
- When you feel overwhelmed, take a break and come back calm and clear-headed.

Gottman also cautions that the presence of "The Four Horsemen"—criticism, contempt, defensiveness, and stonewalling—predicts the breakdown of relationships. Replacing these patterns with the following will teach you how to resolve with grace:

- Starting conversations gently rather than criticizing
- Appreciation rather than contempt
- Accepting accountability rather than defending
- Self-calming as opposed to stonewalling

Steer Clear of Contempt and Defensiveness

The most damaging of the "Four Horsemen" is contempt. It conveys superiority and disdain. Eye-rolling, sarcasm, and mockery can seriously damage your spouse's self-esteem. Couples who repeatedly communicate contempt and disrespect are less likely to experience emotional safety, trust, and mutual appreciation in their relationship (Gottman and Silver 1999).

Defensiveness, on the other hand, is frequently self-protective, yet impedes understanding. When one partner becomes defensive, they stop listening and begin reacting. The cycle continues, and love fades.

To stay away from these traps:

- Practice gratitude on a regular basis, focusing on what your partner does well.
- Apologize without adding qualifiers: "I am sorry I hurt you," not "I am sorry you feel that way."

- Choose humility over pride and grace over blaming.

Ellen White reminds us,

"Neither the husband nor the wife should attempt to exercise over the other an arbitrary control. Do not try to compel each other to yield to your wishes. You cannot do this and retain each other's love. Be kind, patient, forbearing, considerate, and courteous. By the grace of God, you can succeed in making each other happy, as in your marriage vow you promised to do" (*The Adventist Home*, 118).

Communication as Love and Respect in Action

Communication is where love and respect are expressed. For men, respect frequently manifests as being heard without correction or scorn. And empathy and verbal confirmation are how women perceive love.

Couples that speak each other's love language have fewer disagreements and more affection. Respectful discourse develops bridges, whereas contemptuous language creates walls.

Practical Communication Rituals

Couples can cultivate healthy communication through intentional rituals, such as:

- **Daily Check-ins:** Ask each other, "What was the best and hardest part of your day?"
- **Weekly Heart Talks:** Set aside 30–60 minutes for undistracted connection.
- **Prayer Before Conflict**: Inviting God into difficult conversations changes the atmosphere.

- **A Communication Covenant**: A Communication Covenant is a *mutual agreement* between two people—usually a couple—about how they will speak, listen, and handle conversations, especially during difficult moments. It may include daily affirmations and/or guidelines to respect timeouts, not interrupt, or not use sarcasm.

These activities raise communication from ordinary to ritual, with each word planting the seeds of intimacy.

Final Thoughts

Healthy communication is the foundation of a successful marriage. Couples who listen with their hearts, talk with grace, and resolve with humility mirror Christ's character in their homes. As you journey through love and respect, let every conversation be a prayer—an offering of peace, patience, and purpose.

Reflection and Assessment Guide

Reflection Questions
- On a scale of 1–10, how well do you feel heard in your relationship?
- How do you usually respond when your spouse is upset? Do you listen or react?
- In what ways have you unintentionally used criticism or contempt in your communication?
- When was the last time you genuinely apologized without being defensive?
- How can you make listening a more sacred and intentional act in your daily life?

Couple Conversation Starters

- I feel most loved/respected by you when you say or do…
- One thing I need from you during conflict that helps me feel safe is…
- What can we do to improve how we listen to each other?
- What rules or boundaries should we create for arguing fairly?
- Let's choose one day each week to practice a new communication habit. What should we start with?

Communication Health Assessment

Read each statement and score honestly based on your recent experiences. Use the following scale:

1 (Never), 2 (Rarely), 3 (Sometimes), 4 (Often), 5 (Always)

No.	Statement	Score
1	I listen without interrupting when my spouse speaks.	
2	I validate my spouse's feelings even if I don't agree with them.	
3	We use "I" statements instead of blaming language.	
4	I avoid sarcasm or contempt in our conversations.	
5	We discuss conflicts calmly and respectfully.	
6	I apologize sincerely when I am wrong.	
7	We give each other space and time to cool off if needed during conflict.	
8	We practice daily or weekly check-ins to stay connected.	
9	I speak words of affirmation and appreciation to my spouse.	

10	We invite God into our communication and decision-making.	

Total Score: _____ / 50

Score Interpretation:

- 41–50: *Excellent Communication*—Your relationship exhibits strong patterns of loving and respectful communication. Keep building on these habits!
- 31–40: *Healthy, with Room to Grow*—You're doing well, but there are some areas to tune up. Focus on improving weaker spots and being more consistent.
- 21–30: *Needs Attention*—Communication challenges may be affecting your intimacy. Consider setting time aside to work through recurring issues with grace.
- 10–20: *High Risk Zone*—Your communication is most likely strained and potentially destructive. When the need arises, consider seeking pastoral counseling, a qualified therapist, or a reputable mentor couple.

Prayer Focus

"Lord, teach us to listen with our hearts. May our words bring healing and not harm. Help us speak in love and seek peace in our disagreements. Make our communication a channel of Your grace in our marriage. Amen."

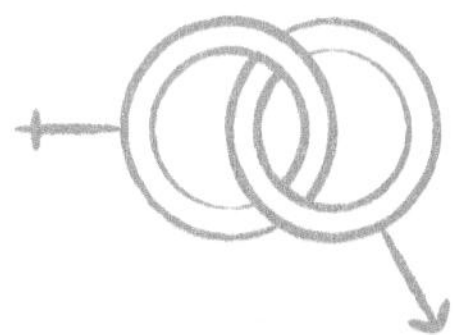

Chapter 7:

SACRED SURRENDER—MUTUAL SUBMISSION AND SHARED RESPONSIBILITY IN MARRIAGE

"Submit to one another out of reverence for Christ."
Ephesians 5:21, NIV

The word *submission* has often stirred tension in conversations about marriage. To some, it suggests passivity or inequality. Yet in Scripture, mutual sub-mission is not about power—it is about partnership. It's a call to humble service, a divine design where both husband and wife are invited to surrender their egos, not their identities, in a dance of love and respect.

During the pandemic, when traditional gender roles were blurred by remote work, homeschooling, and shared domestic life, many couples found themselves renegotiating responsibilities. Some thrived; others wrestled with resentment and imbalance. This chapter explores what it means to walk together as co-heirs of grace, sharing the burdens and blessings of life with mutual honor and trust.

Biblical Foundations of Mutual Submission

Ephesians 5:21–33 remains one of the most widely discussed—and often misunderstood—passages concerning marriage. But at the start of this passage is a verse that frames everything that follows:

"Submit to one another out of reverence for Christ" (Ephesians 5:21, NIV).

This is a verse we often skip past, but it is the key that unlocks the meaning of the rest. Mutual submission is not about power; it is about posture. It's not about who is in charge; it's about who is willing to serve. In the original Greek, the verb *hupotassō* (to submit) implies a voluntary yielding—not one born from coercion or inferiority, but from love, humility, and Christ-centered devotion.

The Model Is Jesus

Jesus, though Lord of all, humbled Himself. He washed the feet of His disciples (John 13:5). He touched lepers (Mark 1:41). He forgave sinners (Luke 7:47–50). He laid down His life not only for His friends but also for those who betrayed Him. This kind of submission is not weakness—it's the most courageous form of love the world has ever known.

Paul goes on to say,

"Husbands, love your wives, just as Christ loved the church and gave himself up for her" (Ephesians 5:25, NIV).

This is not a call to control—it's a call to crucifixion. A husband is invited into a daily, living sacrifice for the good of his wife, just as Christ gave Himself for us. He is not lord over her; he is called to *love her unto death*. And wives are invited into a posture of honoring and supporting this self-giving leadership—not because their husbands are always right, but because they are choosing to reflect the church's trust in Christ's redeeming care:

"The wife must respect her husband" (Ephesians 5:33, NIV).

In this passage, Paul isn't establishing a chain of command; he's painting a portrait of Christlike devotion. It's not *him over her* or *her under him—it's each for the other,* both under Christ.

As Ellen White reminds us,

"Neither husband nor wife is to make a plea for rulership. The Lord has laid down the principle that is to guide in this matter. The husband is to cherish his wife as Christ cherishes the church. And the wife is to respect and love her husband" (*The Adventist Home*, 106, 107).

That's not just doctrine; it's discipleship. In real life, this looks like a husband listening even when he feels tired and a wife encouraging even when she feels discouraged. It's the sacred dance of grace, where each partner lays down pride, picks up love, and carries the cross—not just for their own sake, but for the flourishing of the other.

Mutual submission, then, is not merely a command—it's a calling. A call to be like Jesus in our most intimate human relationship. A call to daily acts of tenderness, deference, and devotion.

This is not outdated theology. It is timeless love.

White also wrote,

"Neither the husband nor the wife should attempt to exercise over the other an arbitrary control. Do not try to compel each other to yield to your wishes. You cannot do this and retain each other's love" (*The Ministry of Healing*, 361).

Mutual submission means that decisions are made together, that each partner listens and leads with Christ-centered selflessness.

Psychological Dimensions of Shared Responsibility

Dr. John Gottman's research indicates that in thriving heterosexual marriages, husbands who are willing to accept influence from their wives tend to have happier, more stable relationships (Gottman and Silver 1999, 100–125).

A Pew Research Center analysis found that a majority of married adults (56%) view sharing household chores as very important to a successful marriage, with perceptions of equal division more common in dual-earner homes (Pew Research Center 2016).

Risman and Davis (2013, 733–755) argue that shifting from "sex roles" to **gender structures** means rethinking how we assign tasks in the home and leadership in the relationship. Instead of defaulting to tradition, we ask, "Who is best equipped, most available, or most passionate about this task?"

The Gift of Shared Leadership

Shared responsibility is not just about chores or finances—it's about **shared vision and leadership**. When a couple co-leads their home, they co-create a life of meaning.

Shared leadership means:

- **Praying together** before making major decisions
- **Setting goals** as a team—spiritually, financially, and relationally
- **Dividing roles** not by tradition but by gifting, availability, and agreement

When one person dominates, the other may feel invisible or resentful. But when both voices are heard and both hearts are honored, marriage becomes a **harmonious duet** rather than a solo performance.

The Healing Power in Humility

In today's individualistic culture, submission may sound offensive. But in Christ, submission is a pathway to healing. It says, "I trust you enough to lean on you. I love you enough to yield."

Mutual submission breaks the cycle of pride and self-protection, inviting grace into every interaction. When couples practice **"I'll go second" love**, they don't insist on having the last word. They ask, "How can I serve you today?" This humble posture is revolutionary—and healing.

Sacred Surrender in Everyday Life

How can couples practice mutual submission and shared responsibility? Here are a few ideas:

- **A "Weekly Roles Talk"**: Take 15 minutes every week to reassess who's handling what and how each person is feeling about it.
- **Gratitude Before Grievance**: Before bringing up a concern, name something your spouse is doing well.

- **The 3–3–3 Rule**: Each partner chooses three things they always do, three they are flexible on, and three things they want to switch up.
- **Couple Devotions with Decision Time**: Pray over roles and decisions together, submitting to God and each other.

Final Thoughts

Marriage is not a power struggle; it's a **sacred surrender**. When love and respect are mutual, so is submission. When leadership is shared, so is the joy. In this divine dance, neither partner leads alone. They move together in rhythm with Christ, each step guided by humility, grace, and shared purpose.

"Two are better than one, because they have a good reward for their labor" (Ecclesiastes 4:9).

Surrender in marriage is not a sign of weakness; rather, it embodies the profound strength of yielding to God's will and each other's love. When two hearts learn to humble themselves, actively listen, and prioritize Christ, a new kind of intimacy emerges—one founded not on control but on unwavering trust.

However, even in our surrender, we may encounter challenges. Misplaced words, unresolved wounds, and brokenness may still surface. Consequently, surrender must be accompanied by grace. In the subsequent chapter, we will delve into the process of repairing damage and rebuilding what has been lost. The beauty of a surrendered marriage lies not in the perfection of the husband and wife but in their willingness to embark on a new journey, guided by God's divine intervention in the restoration process.

Reflection and Assessment Guide

Key Scripture

"Submit to one another out of reverence for Christ" (Ephesians 5:21, NIV).

Ellen G. White Insight

"Neither the husband nor the wife should attempt to exercise over the other an arbitrary control. ... You cannot do this and retain each other's love" (*The Adventist Home*, 118).

Take a moment to meditate and pray over these words, asking God to reveal where mutual submission and shared leadership can be deepened in your marriage.

Reflection Questions

- What does mutual submission mean to you personally?
- Have your views changed over time?
- In what ways do you find it easy—or difficult—to share leadership and responsibility in your relationship?
- How do you typically respond when you feel your voice or contribution is not valued?
- Can you identify a recent moment where either you or your spouse practiced mutual submission? What did you learn from it?
- Are there tasks or responsibilities you've assumed out of habit or tradition that need to be re-evaluated?

Couple Conversation Starters

Set aside time for both partners to share and discuss openly:

1. Do we feel that leadership in our relationship is balanced? If not, where is the imbalance?
2. How do we make decisions—major and minor? Is one person always taking the lead?
3. Are we each clear on our roles and responsibilities? Is there an area where resentment or fatigue may be growing?
4. How can we communicate better about sharing the emotional, spiritual, financial, and domestic load?
5. How can we cultivate a culture of humility, gratitude, and grace in the way we lead each other?

Mutual Submission and Shared Responsibility Assessment Tool

Rate each of the statements, using the following scale:

1 (Rarely True), 2 (Sometimes True), 3 (Often True), 4 (Usually True), 5 (Always True)

Statement	Rating (1–5)
We make decisions together and consider each other's perspectives.	
We regularly communicate about shared responsibilities (chores, finances, parenting, etc.).	
I feel my contributions to the relationship are equally valued.	
We both accept influence from each other and are willing to change.	
We approach conflict with humility and a desire to understand, not dominate.	
There is no pressure for either of us to conform to rigid or traditional gender roles.	

We pray together and seek God's will in decision-making.	
We affirm one another for the roles we play and the sacrifices we make.	
We reassess roles regularly to avoid imbalance or burnout.	
Our relationship reflects Christlike humility and mutual service.	

Total Score: _______ / 50

Score Interpretation:

- **45–50:** *Sacred Partnership*—You are living out a strong model of mutual submission and shared leadership. Keep nurturing this sacred dynamic.
- **35–44:** *Growing Mutuality*—You are on a solid path but may benefit from more intentional communication and role clarification.
- **25–34:** *Needs Rebalancing*—Consider re-evaluating the way leadership and responsibility are distributed in your home. Discuss honestly and lovingly.
- **Below 25:** *Strained Dynamics*—You may be experiencing relational imbalance. Seek wise counsel, and consider practical changes to restore equity and connection.

Action Plan: Practices for Sacred Surrender

Choose 1–3 of the following to implement this week:

- Hold a 15-minute "Weekly Roles Talk" to clarify who does what and how each of you is feeling.
- Use the "3–3–3 Rule" to reassess tasks and preferences: three

tasks you always want, three you're flexible about, and three you'd like to switch.

- Pray together before a major decision, seeking mutual discernment.
- Express appreciation for one thing your spouse is doing each day.
- Read Ephesians 5:21–33 together and reflect on what mutual submission looks like in your context.

Marriage is not about who leads and who follows—it's about who serves and who sacrifices, side by side, under the headship of Christ.

In the divine dance of marriage, mutual submission is not weakness but strength. Shared responsibility is not division—it's unity. May your love grow richer as you surrender daily to each other and to the One who binds you together in grace.

Prayer Focus

"Lord, show us how to surrender with grace. Help us to trust those who lead us and to love those who follow us. Help us learn how to share the weight of marriage, not as a hardship but as a gift. In humility and love, may our hearts first yield to You and then to one another. Let our home show how selfless Your grace is."

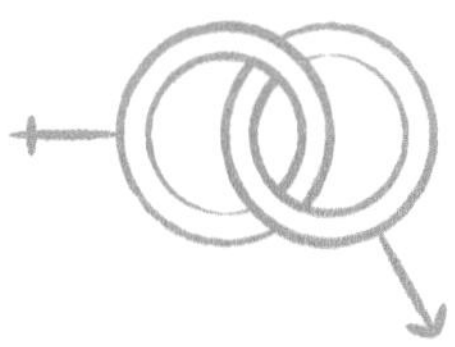

REPAIR AND REBUILDING—THE GRACE OF SECOND CHANCES

"He heals the brokenhearted and binds up their wounds."
Psalm 147:3

No relationship embarks on a journey intending to fall apart. But the truth is that even the healthiest relationships can go through periods of drought, separation, or severe hurt. For many couples, the disintegration of love and respect does not occur in a single instant; rather, neglect, unresolved conflict, and unmet emotional demands gradually erode trust.

However, breakdown does not mean the end. In God's economy, shattered things can be restored. It is possible to reignite love. It is possible to restore respect. This chapter is for the injured, the tired, and those who question, "Can we ever get back what we have lost?"

The Biblical Model for Restoration

Scripture never glosses over the realities of human relation-

99

ships. Love, as God intended, entails two imperfect people learning to live, develop, and heal together. The Bible does not guarantee a pain-free road, but it does promise that God's grace is greater than our brokenness and that His power is perfected in our weakness (2 Corinthians 12:9).

The narrative of the prophet Hosea and his wife, Gomer, is one of the most striking examples of marital reunion. Complete abandonment might have been justified by her serial infidelity. But God commanded Hosea, instead, to do the unimaginable:

"Go again, love a woman who is loved by a lover and is committing adultery" (Hosea 3:1).

This story has to do with God's unfailing love for all disloyal people, not just Hosea and Gomer. Hosea's love became a living parable, showing us that true restoration involves extending grace rather than minimizing pain.

This act of grace-filled restoration was personified by Jesus. Even after Peter rejected him three times, Jesus did not abandon him. Reminiscent of the fire by which Peter rejected Him, He met him at the charcoal fire on the beach (John 21:9) and gently restored him while posing the question "Do you love Me?" three times. This was a request to come back rather than a test of loyalty. Biblical restoration is based on a compassionate call back to love rather than a ruthless reprimand.

The same invitation echoes through Isaiah's words,

"'Come now, and let us reason together,' says the LORD. 'Though your sins are like scarlet, they shall be as white as snow'" (Isaiah 1:18).

This is an invitation not only to sinners in general but also to shattered homes, broken relationships, and wounded hearts. What sin has destroyed God wants to rebuild with transformational grace, not with band-aid solutions.

Ellen White offered timely wisdom when she wrote,

"If one errs, the other will exercise Christlike forbearance and not draw coldly away" (*The Adventist Home*, 118).

This counsel deviates from culturally normative practices. The phrase "walk away if it hurts" is frequently employed. However, the Bible instructs,

"Bear with each other and forgive one another if any of you has a grievance against someone. Forgive as the Lord forgave you" (Colossians 3:13, NIV).

Denying the offense's occurrence isn't restoration. Restoration necessitates acknowledging the pain, presenting it at the foot of the cross, and permitting God to resurrect the offender into a more honorable individual.

Forgiveness isn't forgetting; it's the decision to not let the past imprison you. It is deciding to put faith above fear, love above retribution, and mercy above resentment. While it does not change the past, forgiveness does pave the way for a future that has been redeemed. When a couple chooses to mend rather than retaliate, they are engaging in the holy task of reconciliation—the very mission that Christ came to do (2 Corinthians 5:18). Restoration isn't a side note in marriage—it's the very heart of the gospel lived out between two people.

Recognizing the Ruins: How Marriages Break

In an earlier chapter, we mentioned Dr. Gottman's "Four Horsemen of the Apocalypse": stonewalling, defensiveness, scorn, and criticism. When these actions become routine, they under-mine the bonds of attachment and respect.

As a relationship begins to unravel, the signs of a breakdown can be quiet—but deeply painful. Ellen G. White correctly stated,

> "It is truly noble to forgive and pass over a wrong; but it is mean and cowardly to revenge an injury. Let me entreat you to be above everything like engaging in a dispute, or speaking disrespectfully or sneeringly of those who annoy you, and do not respect themselves enough to behave properly" (*An Appeal to the Youth*, 65).

However, when the signs of a breakdown are absent, the consequences can also be disastrous. Communication that is angry, defensive, or nonexistent might be a warning sign of a troubled relationship. When bad communication habits become entrenched, they can cause emotional retreat or apathy, leaving partners feeling alienated and unvalued.

Persistent feelings of contempt, bitterness, or emotional distance often signal that a relationship is under strain. But these surface emotions are usually symptoms of something deeper. As social researcher Brené Brown explains, "shame and fear are the source of most of our disconnection" (2012, 123). When partners begin to feel inadequate, misunderstood, or emotionally unsafe, shame and fear can quietly take root. Over time, this leads to withdrawal, mistrust, and a loss of intimacy—both physical and spiritual. As Ellen White so beautifully stated,

> "Marriage, a union for life, is a symbol of the union between Christ and His church" (*The Faith I Live By*, 259).

When this love is missing, the relationship can feel hollow and unsatisfactory.

Regardless of the harm done, restoring a relationship is achie-vable when both partners are ready to put in the effort. As psychologist Sue Johnson put it, "Love is not just a feeling, but a choice—a choice to prioritize the relationship and work through the tough times" (2013, 156). This necessitates a commitment to communicate effectively, listen actively, and make amends as needed. Couples can begin to restore their relationship and create a stronger, more durable bond by recognizing signs of breakdown and taking action to resolve them.

Psychological Insights: Why Forgiveness and Counseling Matter

Forgiveness isn't just spiritual—it's also profoundly healing. Unforgiveness often fuels anxiety, distance, and emotional exhaustion. But when forgiveness begins—sometimes slowly, sometimes with tears—it creates space for peace, empathy, and reconnection. Research confirms what the gospel has always revealed: letting go of resentment reduces stress and allows love to breathe again (Wade et al. 2014).

Rebuilding trust takes time. It often starts when two people, still hurting but still hopeful, choose to try again—with God's help and a heart willing to grow. It involves honest conversations free from blame, a willingness to truly listen, and a safe space to be real. Empathy grows when both partners seek to understand each other. Even in emotional uncertainty, shared commitment matters.

Sometimes, lasting repair requires outside support like counseling, mentoring, or prayer. Counseling can help couples find clarity, offer forgiveness, and reconnect in meaningful ways. Rebuilding takes humility, patience, and God's grace—one step at a time.

The Grace of Second Chances

Some marriages fail because of hurt rather than hatred. Grace serves as a bridge between hearts that have drifted apart. Giving a second opportunity to your spouse—or receiving one—requires courage, humility, and faith.

Grace, however, does not imply condoning abuse or repeated betrayal. It means making space for transformation—when the husband and wife are receptive. Restoration occurs when each says, "I would like to try again," "I want to improve," or "Let us rebuild."

Practical Tools for Rebuilding

- **The Apology Inventory:** Each couple determines what it takes to truly apologize to the other.
- **Weekly Check-ins:** Once a week, have 30-minute conversations to examine emotional connection, stress, and support.
- **The Forgiveness Letter:** Write a letter to each other explaining what you are releasing and what you expect to accomplish.
- **Rituals of Rebuilding:** Rekindle intimacy via shared prayer, date nights, and affirmations.

Sacred Restoration: God's Role in the Process

God not only heals individuals, but also restores relationships. He specializes in resurrection. As we surrender to Him, He can transform ashes into beauty (Isaiah 61:3). When love and respect are harmed, the Spirit of God provides the means for repair:

- Love that bears everything (1 Corinthians 13)
- Peace that surpasses understanding (Philippians 4:7)
- Wisdom from above that is peaceful and merciful (James 3:17)

Rebuilding a broken marriage is more than just returning to what was; it is also a re-creation of what can be, thanks to grace. When trust is broken and closeness disappears, the goal should not be to just patch up existing structures but to build something new that is stronger and more beautiful than before. Grace empowers partners to confront difficult realities, extend forgiveness, and construct a new story that is defined by redemptive possibility rather than previous mistakes. Just as God does not just restore sinners to their former state but transforms them into new creations in Christ (2 Corinthians 5:17), a broken marriage can be transformed into a sacred testimony of healing. This process needs humility, intentionality, and divine intervention, yet it offers the potential for deeper connection, renewed purpose, and shared spiritual progress.

According to Dr. Sue Johnson, "The most functional way to regulate difficult emotions in love relationships is to share them" (2008, 37). Brokenness creates the soil for a new kind of love to flourish when grace and mutual vulnerability are present—a love that is resilient, compassionate, and anchored in Christ.

Final Thoughts

Marriage is about more than just remaining together; it is about growing together, especially during the most difficult times. When love and respect have been shattered, mending may appear unattainable. But God is the source of new beginnings.

Every apology, every effort to improve, and every tear shed in prayer is a step toward building something new. When we allow grace to enter our hearts, second chances become precious opportunities.

Let your love story be about healing. Let your marriage become a quiet testimony of what grace can restore.

"Behold, I make all things new" (Revelation 21:5).

Every couple faces moments when things fall apart—harsh words, long silences, broken trust. But God specializes in new beginnings. With humility, forgiveness, and His relentless grace, what was once fractured can become whole again. In Christ, repair is never the end of the story—it's the sacred beginning of something stronger, deeper, and beautifully new.

Repair is not the end of the story—it is the beginning of something redemptive. As walls come down and hearts soften, the seeds of a new legacy are planted. In the next chapter, we'll explore how healed marriages become living testimonies—how the choices you make today to forgive, stay, and grow can leave behind a legacy of love that outlives you and blesses generations to come. Restored love, rooted in grace, leaves the most beautiful mark.

Reflection and Assessment Guide

Reflection Questions
- **When Love Hurts:** Reflect on a time in your relationship when you felt emotionally disconnected or deeply hurt. What led to that season, and how did you respond to it?
- **Signs of Breakdown:** Do any of the Four Horsemen (criticism, contempt, defensiveness, and stonewalling) show

up in your communication patterns? Which one do you struggle with the most, and how might it be affecting your marriage?

- **Owning the Ruins:** Are there areas where you've contributed to the breakdown of love and respect in your marriage? How willing are you to take responsibility and seek forgiveness?
- **Experiencing Grace:** How do you understand the concept of "second chances" in light of God's grace? Can you think of a moment when you or your spouse extended forgiveness that brought healing?
- **Hope and Hesitation:** What fears or hopes do you have about rebuilding your relationship after hurt or conflict? What role do you believe God wants to play in that process?

Couple Conversation Starters

- What does forgiveness look like for each of us? How can we create a safe space for apologies and change?
- How have we responded to breakdowns in the past, and what would we like to do differently going forward?
- What are some "rituals of repair" we can adopt (e.g., weekly check-ins, grace-filled conversations, rebuilding dates)?
- In what ways can we invite God into our healing journey— through prayer, devotionals, or seeking spiritual mentorship?

Marriage Assessment Tool: Rebuilding Together

Evaluate the statements, using the following scale:

1 (Rarely True), 2 (Sometimes True), 3 (Often True), 4 (Usually True), 5 (Always True)

Statement	1	2	3	4	5
We talk openly and calmly about our relationship struggles.					
We actively practice forgiveness and avoid bringing up past mistakes.					
Both of us are willing to seek help (counseling, mentorship, etc.).					
We prioritize spiritual healing and prayer in our relationship.					
We are intentional about rebuilding trust and respect through action.					

Reflection: What do your responses reveal? Highlight one area you feel strong in and one that needs healing.

Action Plan: This Week's Healing Step

Choose *one* of the following:

- Write a forgiveness letter to your spouse.
- Schedule a counseling session or talk to a trusted couple.
- Create a "Let's Try Again" date night to reset your emotional connection.
- Have a 15-minute prayer together each day, focused on healing and grace.

Journal your experience: What did this step teach you about yourself, your spouse, and your relationship with God?

Prayer Focus

"Create in me a clean heart, O God, and renew a right spirit within me" (Psalm 51:10).

Pray together:

"Lord, where we have hurt and been hurt, give us courage to heal. Teach us to forgive as You have forgiven us. Renew our love, rebuild our trust, and restore what has been broken. May our marriage reflect Your mercy, and may Your grace be the foundation of our second chance. Amen."

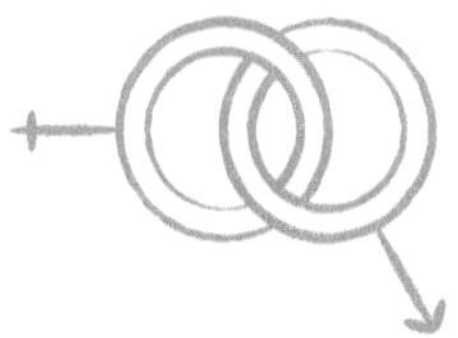

THE LEGACY OF LOVE—BUILDING A MARRIAGE THAT LASTS FOR GENERATIONS

"His mercy extends to those who fear him, from generation to generation." Luke 1:50, NIV

Marriage is so much more than just sharing a house or changing your last name. At its core, it's a legacy—a sacred trust passed down that can shape the emotional, spiritual, and relational world of everyone who comes after. The way a husband and wife speak to each other, forgive each other, and hold on to each other through life's chaos—that becomes a story the children absorb, the grandchildren remember, and sometimes, entire communities feel.

We live in a time when everything moves fast, and people are told to chase dreams alone. So, when you see a couple who are still choosing each other—through illness, financial strain, or just the wear and tear of ordinary days—it almost stops you in your tracks. That kind of love speaks louder than any fairy-tale ending. It reminds us that real love is a steady choice, not a passing emotion.

This chapter is about seeing marriage not just as a current commitment but as a future investment—a lifelong journey anchored in God's faithfulness, shaped by grace, and built to bless generations we may never meet.

Marriage: A Covenant, Not Just a Contract

Somewhere along the way, culture started selling us a lighter version of marriage, one where love is only worth holding onto if it stays convenient or exciting. Relationships began to be viewed like subscriptions—cancel anytime if you're no longer satisfied.

That mindset has crept into how many see marriage today: a deal with conditions. "I'll give my best as long as you meet my expectations." It's protective. It plans for exits. It avoids pain.

But God's blueprint for marriage doesn't look like that at all. Scripture shows us something deeper—something much more sacred. Marriage, in God's eyes, isn't a contract to adjust when things get hard. It's a *covenant*. And a covenant says: "I'm not leaving when it gets uncomfortable. I'm staying because I promised."

Covenants are built on faithfulness, not convenience. They're held together not by perfect circumstances but by grace—grace that shows up when tempers are short, when the bills are overdue, when love feels more like a choice than a feeling. And this covenant? It's not just between two people. God Himself is in the room, bearing witness.

The prophet Malachi speaks to this with raw honesty:

"The LORD has been witness between you and the wife of your youth, with whom you have dealt treacherously;

yet she is your companion and your wife by covenant" (Malachi 2:14).

Let that sink in. God isn't sitting on the sidelines, casually observing. He's a witness to every whispered vow, every tear-filled reconciliation, and every quiet act of staying. When Malachi calls her "your *companion*," that's not a cold legal term. That's the person who held your hand in the emergency room. The one who stayed up with you when the baby wouldn't sleep. The one who saw your worst moments—and didn't walk away.

This kind of bond can't be measured by feelings alone. It's shaped by the grace of a God who stays—and teaches us to stay too.

Violating that covenant not only causes harm to the individual, but it also grieves God. In biblical theology, the term *covenant* (Hebrew: *berith*) alludes to God's steadfast commitment to His people, despite their flaws and rebellion. God's covenants are based on fidelity rather than emotion. His promises hold even when ours falter. Marriage is intended to symbolize heavenly love.

As we have seen all throughout this book, the apostle Paul affirms this notion in Ephesians 5:25, writing,

"Husbands, love your wives as Christ also loved the church and gave Himself for her."

This chapter uses covenantal terminology to emphasize that Christ's love for us was not based on our ease of being loved, but rather on a profound and costly sacrifice. It was a sacrificial and redemptive love, and we are required to embody it in marriage. While perfection is impossible to achieve, continuous love is required, and covenantal faithfulness should serve as the foundation.

Ellen White adds this insight:

"Marriage is something that will influence and affect your life both in this world and in the world to come" (*The Adventist Home*, 43).

When we perceive marriage as a covenant, it profoundly influences our interactions with one another, our capacity for forgiveness, our resilience in facing adversity, and our celebration of achievements. It transforms ordinary moments into sacred experiences—folding laundry, offering prayers for children, prioritizing peace over the pursuit of argumentation.

Covenantal marriage says, "I reaffirm my commitment to you today—not because it is effortless or flawless, but because I made a solemn vow and the presence of God sustains us."

When two individuals establish a marriage based on a covenant—on enduring love, divine grace, and mutual sacrifice—they leave behind not only cherished memories but also a lasting legacy of faithfulness that will resonate through generations. This eternal perspective profoundly transforms the dynamics of marriage. If marriage were solely concerned with mutual happiness, it would be understandable to seek separation when happiness diminishes. However, if it is a divine covenant—a symbol of Christ's unwavering love for His bride, the church—it transforms into a compelling call to remain, to forgive, to grow, and to serve.

Jesus doesn't abandon His church when she fails. He restores her. Likewise, a covenantal marriage says, "Even when it's hard, I am here—not because it's easy, but because God has bound us together."

Consider the language of Hosea, when God instructed the prophet to rekindle his love for his unfaithful wife, mirroring His own covenantal love for Israel:

"The LORD said to me, 'Go, show your love to your wife again, though she is loved by another man and is an adulteress. Love her as the LORD loves the Israelites, though they turn to other gods and love the sacred raisin cakes'" (Hosea 3:1, NIV).

This is not sentimentality; it is radical grace. Marriage was inherently intended to embody the gospel: grace when undeserved, mercy when inconvenient, and love when it entails significant sacrifice. This does not imply enduring abuse or facilitating harm. However, it does entail establishing a relationship not on the precarious foundation of mutual performance but on the steadfast foundation of spiritual commitment.

In the words of Jesus,

"So they are no longer two, but one flesh. Therefore, what God has joined together, let no one separate" (Matthew 19:6, NIV).

To view marriage as a covenant entails a shift from self-preservation to self-sacrifice. It involves perceiving one's spouse not merely as a contractual partner but as a fellow journeyman in a sacred quest—admittedly imperfect, yet divinely chosen to accompany one in grace.

Psychological Patterns Passed Down

Psychological research corroborates that parents' conflict management, affection, and respect provide a template for children's relationships (Gottman, Katz, and Hooven 1996, 2786–88).

A study published in the *Journal of Marriage and Family* (Amato and DeBoer 2001, 1038–1051) demonstrated that children raised in high-conflict marriages, even when their parents remained together, frequently experienced anxiety, trust issues, and challenges in their own marital relationships. In contrast, children from households characterized by respect and love exhibited elevated levels of emotional stability and relational fulfillment in adulthood.

Every decision made within a marriage—whether it involves communication, apologies, or prioritizing each other—forms the foundation that our children and others will either build upon or attempt to recover from.

Sociological Impact: Marriage as a Social Institution

Risman (2013, 733–755) argues that marriage shapes not only families but societies. Healthy marriages contribute to community stability, economic strength, and the socialization of children. When couples invest in each other, they're also investing in the wellbeing of their neighborhoods and nations.

During the pandemic, when couples were confined to the home, researchers noticed a sharp divide: some relationships crumbled under stress, while others deepened through intentionality and spiritual connection. The difference? Those who had built a culture of empathy, flexibility, and shared spiritual values tended to thrive.

Practical Steps for Leaving a Legacy

1. **Create a Family Mission Statement:** Just as companies define their vision, couples can articulate their spiritual and relational goals. Ask:

     - What kind of family do we want to be?
     - What values guide our decisions?
     - How do we want to be remembered?

2. **Celebrate Milestones:** Anniversaries, achievements, baptisms, and family traditions reinforce the story of your love. They create a shared narrative that shapes how your family remembers and models love.

3. **Mentor Other Couples:** Marriage is not just for your benefit. Titus 2 encourages older couples to teach the younger. Sharing your journey—the highs and lows—can offer hope and wisdom to those just starting out.

4. **Forgive and Heal:** Generational patterns of pain don't have to continue. Couples who seek forgiveness, both human and divine, become conduits of healing across generations.

A Sacred Calling for the Future

Leaving a legacy isn't about perfection—it's about faithfulness. It's about showing up, loving well, and making Christ the center of your relationship. A legacy marriage isn't always loud; often, it's the quiet faithfulness of ordinary days lived with extraordinary grace.

As Ellen White wrote,

"Without mutual forbearance and love no earthly power can hold you and your husband in the bonds of Christian unity. Your companionship in the marriage relation should be close and tender, holy and elevated, breathing a spiritual power into your lives, that you may be everything to each other that God's word requires. When you reach the condition that the Lord desires you to reach, you will find heaven below and God in your life" (*The Adventist Home*, 112).

Final Thoughts

Marriage is not the end of your story—it's the beginning of someone else's. By choosing love, respect, forgiveness, and faith, you're not just writing your own chapter; you're preparing a blessing for those yet to be born.

So hold hands. Pray together. Forgive often. And remember: the divine dance of love and respect echoes beyond your lifetime.

"But the steadfast love of the LORD is from everlasting to everlasting on those who fear him, and his righteousness to children's children" (Psalm 103:17, ESV).

Reflection and Assessment Guide

Reflection Questions
- When you think of your marriage, what kind of legacy do you believe you're currently building?
- What do you hope your children, family members, or community will remember about your relationship?
- Identify a few defining moments in your marriage. How did you handle them?
- Were these moments marked by love, grace, or conflict? What do you want to do differently moving forward?
- How has your spiritual walk with God shaped your marriage so far?
- Are there habits you need to strengthen (e.g., praying together, reading Scripture, family worship)?

Couple Conversation Starters

Set aside quiet, uninterrupted time with your spouse to discuss the following questions:

1. **Shared Vision**
   - What are the core values that shape our marriage?
   - If we had to write a family mission statement, what would we want it to include?

2. **Repairing Generational Patterns**
   - Are there any harmful patterns from our family backgrounds that we are repeating in our marriage?
   - How can we work together to break those cycles and create new, healthy patterns?

3. **Intentional Traditions**
   - What small habits or traditions can we create or revive to build strong memories for future generations?

4. **Long-Term Impact**
   - How would we like to support or mentor younger couples in our church or community?

Self-Assessment: How Are We Doing?

Honestly assess your relationship in the below areas, using the following scale:

1 (Never), 2 (Rarely), 3 (Sometimes), 4 (Often), 5 (Always)

Area of Legacy	Score (1–5)	Notes/Action Steps
We prioritize long-term thinking in our relationship.		
We talk about our family's spiritual and moral values.		
We actively work on healing past hurts and generational wounds.		

We model healthy conflict resolution and affection to our children/family.		
We have regular spiritual practices that nurture our marriage.		
We mentor or encourage other couples when possible.		

Reflection Prompt: Review your scores together. Which area are you strongest in? Which one needs more prayer, focus, and growth?

Legacy-Building Action Plan

1. **Create or Revise a Family Mission Statement:** Start with this prompt: "As a couple/family, we exist to..."
2. **Set a Legacy Goal for This Year:** What's one thing you want to start or improve (e.g., weekly prayer night, journaling family stories, mentoring a young couple)?
3. **Journal This Together:** If our grandchildren asked what kept our marriage strong, what would we tell them?

Prayer Focus

"Lord, help us to live and love not just for today, but for eternity. Teach us to forgive as You forgive, to lead with grace, and to plant seeds of righteousness for generations to come. May our marriage reflect Your faithfulness and bless all who come after us. Amen."

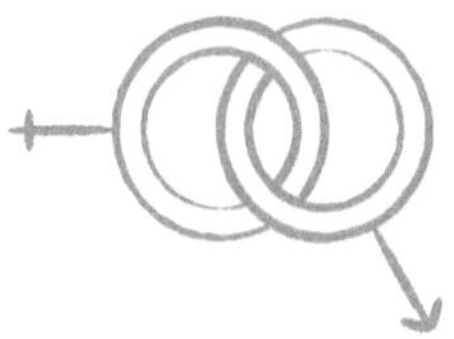

Chapter 10

A MARRIAGE THAT REFLECTS GOD

"But from everlasting to everlasting the LORD's love is with those who fear him, and his righteousness with their children's children—with those who keep his covenant and remember to obey his precepts." Psalm 103:17–18, NIV

A God-centered marriage is not limited to the beauty of the wedding day or the vows exchanged before witnesses. It stretches into the unglamorous days of ordinary life—in seasons of joy, sorrow, triumph, and struggle. It is not merely about companionship; it is about testimony. Every couple, whether intentionally or not, leaves a legacy. The real question is not *if* we will leave one, but *what kind* we will leave behind.

When rooted in Christ, a marriage has the power to echo beyond the walls of the home—touching children, extended family, community, and even church. Ellen White emphasized the home's societal role:

"The heart of the community, of the church, and of the nation is the household" (*The Adventist Home*, 15).

That means marriage is more than a private covenant—it is a public witness.

In this chapter, we explore how a God-centered marriage reflects Christ not only for a lifetime, but in a way that points others to eternal truths. It becomes a ministry of presence, a sermon of grace, and a legacy that inspires others to walk in faith and love.

1. A Living Example: Modeling God's Character at Home

The first place where marriage preaches the gospel is in the home. Long before children grasp doctrinal truths, they absorb the daily rhythm of love, respect, conflict resolution, and grace. Even couples without children still communicate something spiritual through the tone, habits, and holiness of their home life.

A marriage that reflects God models humility, apology, patience, affection, and mutual respect. As Deuteronomy 6:6–7 encourages, we are to talk about God's ways "when you sit in your house, when you walk by the way, when you lie down, and when you rise up." In other words, the home is a living classroom for faith.

Psychologically, children form their first impressions of safety, love, and even God's nature from what they experience at home. According to Amato, stable family structures with effective parenting strongly predict children's cognitive, social, and emotional well-being (Amato 2005, 75–96). Spiritually, Ellen White affirmed,

"In the formation of character, no other influences count
so much as the influence of the home" (*Education*, 283).

When spouses worship together, forgive regularly, and serve one another with joy, they create a spiritual environment that nurtures secure attachment—both to people and to God. These are the roots of a godly legacy.

2. Sharing the Journey: Discipleship Through Marriage

Marriage was never meant to be lived in isolation. Couples who reflect Christ in their love are uniquely positioned to walk alongside others, not as perfect examples, but as living testimonies of grace.

Mentorship in marriage isn't about having all the answers; it's about saying, "We've walked this road. Let's journey together." This is biblical discipleship in relational form. As Paul instructed Timothy,

> "What you have heard from me…entrust to faithful [people] who will be able to teach others also" (2 Timothy 2:2, ESV).

Studies show marriage education improves communication, relationship quality, and satisfaction (Hawkins et al. 2022, 39–64). Whether through structured mentoring or informal friendships, couples who mentor others multiply their impact and allow their marriage to become a vessel of spiritual growth for others.

3. A Daily Witness: Marriage as a Gospel Parable

Paul called marriage a "profound mystery" that reflects Christ's covenant with the church (Ephesians 5:25, 32, NIV). This makes marriage more than a personal blessing—it becomes a parable of grace.

Your marriage may be the only Bible someone reads. Your patience may restore someone's hope. Your humility may invite someone to trust again. In every mundane interaction—how we speak, serve, forgive, and show up—we offer a glimpse of divine love.

Research supports that spiritual intimacy between spouses strongly predicts marital satisfaction and positive relational dynamics (Mahoney et al. 2021, 552–558).

4. Faithfulness in the Ordinary: How God Shines Through the Everyday

Legacy isn't written in dramatic moments but in the daily choices made behind closed doors. What matters most is often what no one else sees: the kind word instead of the cold shoulder, the prayer offered instead of the grudge held, the effort to reconnect instead of withdrawing.

Charles Duhigg observes that repeated patterns shape systems—and systems shape culture (2012, 97–126). In marriage, those small habits of grace form the bedrock of legacy.

Psalm 112:1–2 says,

"Blessed are those who fear the LORD. ... Their children will be mighty in the land" (NIV).

Whether or not children are present, our consistent walk of faithfulness becomes a message to the world. Matthew L. Jacobson states, "Your marriage is the gospel you are preaching to your children" (2019).

5. The Eternal Weight of Faithful Love

A marriage rooted in Christ echoes beyond this life. Though imperfect, it becomes part of the redemptive work God is doing in the world. As Daniel 12:3 declares,

"Those who are wise will shine like the brightness of the heavens, and those who lead many to righteousness, like the stars for ever and ever."

Every surrendered decision, every word spoken in grace, every trial endured together becomes part of heaven's record. Ellen White put it simply:

"The marriage vow links the destinies of the two individuals with bonds which nought but the hand of death should sever" (*Testimonies for the Church* 4, 507).

A Christ-centered marriage becomes more than a relationship. It becomes a ministry. It becomes a sanctuary. And it becomes a lasting witness to the goodness of God.

Reflection and Assessment Guide

Reflection Questions
- How has your understanding of a gospel-centered marriage changed through this chapter?
- In what ways does your marriage reflect God's character daily? Where can you grow in showing grace or humility?
- Have you ever been mentored or discipled by another couple? Are you open to doing the same for someone else?
- How do your home habits model love and respect?
- What spiritual practices can you and your spouse develop to draw closer to Christ together?

Self-Assessment Checklist

Legacy Practice	Always	Sometimes	Rarely	Never
We teach biblical values through words and example.	☐	☐	☐	☐
We pray together regularly.	☐	☐	☐	☐
We offer forgiveness freely.	☐	☐	☐	☐
We support or mentor younger couples.	☐	☐	☐	☐
We engage in spiritual disciplines together.	☐	☐	☐	☐
We intentionally build a God-honoring home culture.	☐	☐	☐	☐
Our marriage reflects joy, patience, kindness, and faith.	☐	☐	☐	☐
We talk about our marriage as a witness.	☐	☐	☐	☐

Legacy Planning Action Steps

1. One area where we want to grow in reflecting Christ:
   ____

2. One step we will take this month to build stronger spiritual connection:
   ____

3. One couple we can encourage or support:
   ____

4. One way our marriage can model God's love more clearly:

5. Our marriage mission statement:

Prayer Focus

"Lord, make our marriage a mirror of Your love. In our daily choices, in our struggles and joys, help us reflect Your grace. May our home be a testimony, our forgiveness a light, and our love a witness to Your faithfulness. Amen."

Bibliography

Amato, Paul R. 2005. "The Impact of Family Formation Change on the Cognitive, Social, and Emotional Well-Being of the Next Generation." *The Future of Children* 15 (2): 75–96.

Amato, Paul R., and Danelle D. DeBoer. 2001. "The Transmission of Marital Instability Across Generations: Relationship Skills or Commitment to Marriage?" *Journal of Marriage and Family* 63 (4): 1038–1051.

American Psychological Association. 2020. *Stress in America 2020: A National Mental Health Crisis.*

Bloch, Lian, Claudia M. Haase, and Robert W. Levenson. 2014. "Emotion Regulation Predicts Marital Satisfaction: More Than a Wives' Tale." *Emotion* 14 (1): 130–44. https://doi.org/10.1037/a0034272.

Bonhoeffer, Dietrich. 1997. *Letters and Papers from Prison.* Touchstone.

Brown, B. 2012. *Daring Greatly: How the Courage to Be Vulnerable Transforms the Way We Live, Love, Parent, and Lead.* Gotham Books.

Chase, Isabella. 2024. "If a Man Feels Disrespected in His Relationship, He'll Often Display These 9 Behaviors." Global English Editing. December 3, 2024. https://geediting.com/if-a-man-feels-disrespected-in-his-relationship-hell-often-display-these-behaviors/.

Duhigg, Charles. 2021. *The Power of Habit: Why We Do What We Do in Life and Business.* Random House.

Eggerichs, Emerson. 2004. *Love and Respect: The Love She Most Desires; The Respect He Desperately Needs.* Thomas Nelson.

Eri, T., T. Tomova Shakur, H. T. Reis, S. Oishi, and E. M. O'Mara.

2024. "Feeling Loved as a Strong Link in Relationship Interactions." *Journal of Personality and Social Psychology.* Advance online publication

Feldhahn, S. 2013. *For Women Only: What You Need to Know About the Inner Lives of Men.* Multnomah Books.

Fincham, F. D., and R.W. May. 2021. "Generalized Gratitude and Prayers of Gratitude in Marriage." *The Journal of Positive Psychology* 16 (2): 282–287. https://doi.org/10.1080/17439760.2020.1716053.

Fisher, Helen. 2006. *Why We Love: The Nature and Chemistry of Romantic Love.* Henry Holt.

Gottman, John, and Nan Silver. 1999. *The Seven Principles for Making Marriage Work.* Three Rivers Press.

Gottman, John, and Nan Silver. 2015. *The Seven Principles for Making Marriage Work.* Harmony.

Gottman, John M., Lynn Fainsilber Katz, and Carole Hooven. 1996. "Parental Meta-Emotion Philosophy and Patterns of Marital Conflict Predict Children's Internalizing and Externalizing Behaviors." *Child Development* 67 (6): 2780–95.

Hawkins, Alan J., David S. Wood, and McKane S. Bean. 2022. "How Effective Are ACF-Funded Couple Relationship Education Programs? A Meta-Analytic Study." *Family Process* 61 (1): 39–64.

Horowitz, Juliana Menasce, Nikki Graf, and Gretchen Livingston. "Marriage and Cohabitation in the U.S." Pew Research Center. November 6, 2019. https://www.pewresearch.org/social-trends/2019/11/06/marriage-and-cohabitation-in-the-u-s/#:~:text=The%20share%20of%20U.S.%20adults,of%20Family%20Growth%20(NSFG).

Jacobson, Matthew L., and Jennifer Smith. 2019. *Marriage After God: Chasing Boldly After God's Purpose for Your Life Together.* Zondervan.

Johnson, Sue M. 2008. *Hold Me Tight: Seven Conversations for a Lifetime of Love.* Little, Brown Spark.

Lachance-Grzela, Mylène, Melissa Ross-Plourde, Marilou Vautour, and Marie-Ève Larocque. 2020. "Mindfulness, Perceived Partner Responsiveness, and Relational Conflict among Emerging Adult Couples." *Canadian Journal of Counselling and Psychotherapy* 54 (3): 435–62.

Lambert, N. M., M. S. Clark, J. Durtschi, F.D. Fincham, and S. M. Graham. 2010. "Benefits of Expressing Gratitude: Expressing Gratitude to a Partner Changes One's View of the Relationship." *Psychological Science* 21 (4): 574–580. https://doi.org/10.1177/0956797610364003.

Mahoney, Annette, Kenneth I. Pargament, and Alfred DeMaris. 2021. "Spiritual Intimacy, Spiritual One-Upmanship, and Marital Conflict Across the Transition to Parenthood." *Journal of Family Psychology* 35 (4): 552–58. https://doi.org/10.1037/fam0000795.

Mangual, Rafael A., Brad Wilcox, Seth Cannon, and Joseph E. Price. 2023. *Stronger Families, Safer Streets.* Institute for Family Studies. https://ifstudies.org/ifs-admin/resources/reports/ifs-strongerfamilies-final-1.pdf.

Markman, H. J., S. M. Stanley, and S. L. Blumberg. 2010. *Fighting for Your Marriage: A Deluxe Revised Edition of the Classic Best-Seller for Enhancing Marriage and Preventing Divorce.* Jossey-Bass.

Murray-Swank, Natalie A., and Kenneth I. Pargament. 2020. "God, Prayer, and the Marriage Covenant: Spiritual Intimacy as a

Predictor of Marital Wellbeing and Witness." *Psychology of Religion and Spirituality* 12 (1): 45–55.

Panganiban, Kimberly. "How To Improve Your Relationship in 24 Hours." The Gottman Institute. Last modified October 10, 2025. https://www.gottman.com/blog/how-to-improve-your-relationship-in-24-hours/.

Pew Research Center. "Sharing Chores a Key to Good Marriage, Say Majority of Married Adults." Pew Research Center, November 30, 2016. https://www.pewresearch.org/short-reads/2016/11/30/sharing-chores-a-key-to-good-marriage-say-majority-of-married-adults/.

Rainey, Dennis. 2002. *Staying Close: Stopping the Natural Drift Toward Isolation in Marriage*. Thomas Nelson.

Reis, H. T. 2013. "Perceived Partner Responsiveness as an Organizing Theme for the Study of Relationships and Well-Being." In *Human Bonding: The Science of Affectional Ties*, edited by M. Mikulincer and P. R. Shaver. Guilford Press, 283–307.

Reis, H. T., M. S. Clark, and J. G. Holmes. 2004. "Perceived Partner Responsiveness as an Organizing Construct in the Study of Intimacy and Closeness." In *Handbook of Closeness and Intimacy*, edited by D. J. Mashek & A. P. Aron. Lawrence Erlbaum Associates Publishers, 201–225.

Risman, Barbara J., and Georgiann Davis. 2013. "From Sex Roles to Gender Structure." *Current Sociology* 61 (5–6): 733–755.

Rogers, Carl R. *A Way of Being*. Boston: Houghton Mifflin, 1980.

Ury, Logan. "Want to Improve Your Relationship? Start Paying More Attention to Bids." The Gottman Institute. Last modified September 19, 2024. https://www.gottman.com/blog/want-to-improve-your-relationship-start-paying-more-attention-to-bids/.

Uvnäs-Moberg, K. 2003. *The Oxytocin Factor: Tapping the Hormone of Calm, Love, and Healing.* Da Capo Press.

Wade, N. G., W. T. Hoyt, J. E. Kidwell, and E. L. Worthington, Jr. 2014. "Efficacy of Psychotherapeutic Interventions to Promote Forgiveness: A Meta-Analysis." *Journal of Consulting and Clinical Psychology,* 82 (1): 154–170.

Waite, Linda J., and Maggie Gallagher. 2000. *The Case for Marriage: Why Married People Are Happier, Healthier, and Better Off Financially.* Broadway Books.

White, Ellen G. 1952. *The Adventist Home.* Review and Herald Publishing Association.

White, Ellen G. 1864. *An Appeal to the Youth.* Seventh-day Adventist Publishing Association.

White, Ellen G. 1903. *Education.* Pacific Press Publishing Association.

White, Ellen G. 1958. *The Faith I Live By.* Review and Herald Publishing Association.

White, Ellen G. 1983. *Letters to Young Lovers.* Pacific Press Publishing Association.

White, Ellen G. 1905. *The Ministry of Healing.* Pacific Press Publishing Association.

White, Ellen G. 1890. *Patriarchs and Prophets.* Review and Herald Publishing Association.

White, Ellen G. 1800. *Testimonies for the Church,* 4. Pacific Press Publishing Association.

White, Ellen G. 1902. *Testimonies for the Church,* 7. Pacific Press Publishing Association.